Canoeing the
Delaware River

Canoeing the Delaware River

Gary Letcher

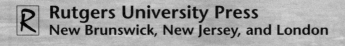
Rutgers University Press
New Brunswick, New Jersey, and London

Library of Congress Cataloging-in-Publication Data

Letcher, Gary, 1952–
    Canoeing the Delaware River / Gary Letcher. — Rev. ed.
      p. cm.
    Includes bibliographical references and index.
    ISBN 0–8135–2450–4 (cloth : alk. paper). — ISBN 0–8135–2451–2
(pbk. : alk. paper)
      1. Canoes and canoeing—Delware River (N.Y.-Del. and N.J.)—
Guidebooks.   2. Delaware River (N.Y.-Del. and N.J.)—Guidebooks.
    3. Canoes and canoeing—Pennsylvania—Guidebooks.
    4. Pennsylvania—Guidebooks.   I. Title.
    GV776.D34L47   1997
    797.1'22'09749—dc21   97–5684
                                                  CIP

Manufactured in the United States of America

This book is dedicated to those with whom I have paddled the Delaware: my wife, Shirley; my son, Ted; my parents, William and Sherry Letcher; my sisters, Donna and Roxanne; my friends Stu Gillard, Bill Goldfarb, Dave Griffin, Zev Kaplan, Courtenay Kling, Gary Lesslie, Rich Messina, Sal Misuraca, Cynthia Poten, Greg Pulis, and Joan Snyder.

Contents

Acknowledgments

This book would not have been possible without the generous assistance of the following people: Roy Given, Chief of Visitor Services, Upper Delaware Scenic and Recreational River; Mary Ann Butler, Port Jervis/Tri-State Chamber of Commerce; C. R. Fauber, Interpretive Specialist, Delaware Water Gap National Recreation Area (DWGNRA); Rab Cika, Supervisory Park Ranger, DWGNRA; Ruth Jones, Proprietor, Kittatinny Canoes; Rick Landers, Bob and Rick Landers' Canoes; Barry Leilich, Chief Naturalist, New Jersey State Park Service; J. Wallis Perry, Pike County Historical Society; Paul Peterson, Chief Engineer, Delaware River Joint Toll Bridge Commission; Ted Day, Regional Engineer, New York Department of Transportation; John Skiba, Chief Engineer, New York Geological Survey; Paul Stern, Superintendent, Delaware and Raritan Canal State Park; Chris Roberts, Public Information Officer, Delaware River Basin Commission; Carney Umphreys, Assistant State Geologist, Pennsylvania Geological Survey; Bill Goldfarb, Cook College professor of environmental studies and angler extraordinaire; and Cynthia Poten, the Delaware Riverkeeper. Special thanks also to Stu Gillard, who assisted with aerial reconnaisance; Courtenay Kling, who assisted with photography and mapping; David Griffin, who assisted with computer services; and my wife, Shirley, who complained just enough that I was spending more time on the river than at home.

I am indebted as well to the following sources: Herbert C. Kraft, *The Archeology of the Tocks Island Area,* for my discussion of Indian artifacts; William F. Henn, *Life Along the Delaware from Bushkill to Milford* (pp. 89–111), for my account of the old bridges at Dingmans Ferry, and his *Westfall Township, Gateway to the West* (pp. 37, 24, 78), for information on Mapes Ferry in Port Jervis, the tale of Sally Decker and her brother, and Dingmans Ferry;

Charles Gilbert Hine, *The Old Mine Road* (pp. 157–158, 153–154), for the incident of Moses Van Campen and the Indian, the origin of the name of Walpack Township, and the history of the Old Mine Road; J. Wallace Hoff, *Two Hundred Miles on the Delaware* (pp. 48, 70, 76, 148), for his descriptions of Narrowsburg, the Roebling Bridge at Lackawaxen, the Delaware and Hudson Canal, and Ringing Rocks. The accounts of the New York and Erie Railroad, the nineteenth-century rafting industry, and the Walking Purchase have drawn on the following works, respectively: Edward Hungerford, *Men of Erie* (pp. 78–81); Harry B. Weiss, *Rafting on the Delaware River* (p. 21); and Clinton Alfred Weslager, *The Delaware Indians* (pp. 188–191).

Author's Notes on the Revised Edition

The first edition of this book was published in 1985, the research having been done mostly in 1982–1983. When the publisher asked for updated listings of services (canoe liveries, campgrounds, eateries, etc.) to be included in a third printing, I suggested that the time had come for a more complete overhaul.

There have been many changes on the river since 1985. Among these changes: new access areas have been developed, and old ones abandoned; new bridges have been built, and some old ones reconstructed; livery businesses have opened, closed, or consolidated; the preliminary plan for the Upper Delaware Scenic and Recreational River was scrapped, and the planning process turned over to the local governments; the National Park Service has assumed a more visible role on the Upper and Middle Delaware; the Tocks Island Dam has been deauthorized, and the Point Pleasant Diversion constructed; the Riverkeeper Network was created as a citizens' advocate for the river; the river water has become even cleaner; Jet Skis have appeared in great number on the river below the water gap (great fun for the riders, but a great nuisance to other river users). But canoeing still remains the most popular way to enjoy the Delaware: the scenery is magnificent, the rapids are more exciting than ever, the wildlife is abundant, and the fish are still biting.

To prepare this revised edition, I canoed the Delaware from Hancock to Trenton, albeit not all in one trip, with several comrades, to verify descriptions noted in the first edition and observe any changes. I interviewed and/or corresponded with dozens of people having knowledge of particular aspects of river use, and consulted many new and recently published sources. This revised edition also contains new photos, and maps that are more readable than those in the first edition (computer graphics have come a long way these last 15 years!). Deleted from this revised edition are listings of restaurants and lodging; for the most part, these change too frequently to be reliably reported. Only "lunch" stops are identified, for example, casual restaurants of long standing within an easy walk from the river. Commercial campgrounds and canoe liveries are listed in the appendix.

Observations, comments, and suggestions may be submitted to me care of the publisher.

Gary R. Letcher

Canoeing the
Delaware River

Introduction

The Plan of the Book

This book is divided into ten sections, each corresponding to a one-day canoe trip on the Delaware River. Each division of the book includes:

1. *introduction*, describing the general characteristics of the river section;
2. *river guide*, a mile-by-mile account of what a canoeist will encounter on the river, including natural features, rapids, structures, historical events, access areas, campgrounds, and riverside lunch spots; and
3. *features*, highlighting points of interest including major rapids, communities, historical events, political controversies, engineering feats, recreational and cultural opportunities, and notable people.

An appendix provides a quick guide to public access areas, rapids, geological, historical, cultural, and recreational highlights, canoe rental services, and campgrounds.

The river guides and map sketches in this book report mileage from the mouth of the Delaware River at Cape May. A reference to "Map 1," "Map 2," and so on, in the "river guides" means that the mileage next described corresponds to that covered by the map. Of course, there are no actual mileposts on the river; a canoeist's position can be determined by reference to natural landmarks, such as islands, rapids, and rock formations, or artificial features, such as bridges, towns, or buildings. The mileage reported in this book corresponds to that reported on recreation maps available from the Delaware River Basin Commission (DRBC). The DRBC first published its maps in 1964, with revised editions published in 1979 and 1991.

Here and there the guide identifies riverside places to lunch, that is, casual restaurants an easy walk from the river that would not object to grungy canoeists dropping in.

The river guide often refers to "eddies" and "rifts." In the vernacular of old-time timber raftsmen, eddies are the slow pools between rifts, or shallows (and often rapids). The raftsmen had names for the important eddies and rifts, and though no longer commonly known, these names are used to the extent possible in this book.

The Delaware River is much more than a body of water flowing from the mountains to the sea: it is the focus of many fascinating places and events. The accounts contained in this book are necessarily brief and therefore incomplete, but they may stimulate readers to make further inquiries.

Canoes, Kayaks, Rafts, and Tubes

The first boats to ply the Delaware River were canoes. For thousands of years the Lenni Lenape Indians and their predecessors paddled hollowed chestnut logs up and down the Delaware for hunting, transportation, and communication. Later, canoes were supplanted by timber rafts, Durham boats, and canal barges as the Delaware became an avenue of commerce.

Then, as the Delaware's commercial appeal waned, a new phenomenon grew on the river: canoes began to return! At first, only a few hardy souls in wood and canvas boats ventured out for fishing or vacation excursions. In 1892 J. Wallace Hoff and four comrades dared to paddle all the way from Balls Eddy to Trenton, a 10-day trip. In 1933, 60 teams of canoeists joined in a Great Canoe Marathon from Easton to Trenton, calling attention to the poor water quality. Mass production of canoes, livery operations, easy access, and improvement in water quality brought an explosion of canoeing to the Delaware. There are now more than 20 canoe outfitters strung from Hancock to Trenton. On any summer day thousands of people may be paddling on the Delaware.

Here is what the River Management Plan for the Upper Delaware Scenic and Recreational River has to say about canoeing on the Delaware:

> The Upper Delaware is one of the most outstanding canoeing rivers in the Northeast. . . . Boating experts have stated that the combination of proximity to major metropolitan areas, high visual quality, and consistent flows due to upstream dam releases make

1. Canoeists approach the Milford Beach access area, maintained by the National Park Service. There are public-access points on the Delaware available for launch and landing of canoes and other boats. Photo by the author.

the Upper Delaware one of the finest recreational canoeing rivers in the Northeast. . . .

Data on river use throughout the United States is incomplete, but many boating experts agree that the Upper Delaware receives more recreational canoeing use than any other river in the northeast, and that it is certainly one of the most popular canoeing rivers in the country. . . .

In other words, people enjoy the Delaware because it is easy to get to, the scenery is spectacular, and the water is clean and plentiful. The Delaware River seems to have been made with canoeing in mind.

In recent years, canoe livery and rental outfitters have added rubber rafts and tubes to their offerings. Indeed, some outfitters would rather rent tubes than canoes: tubes can be carried by the customer, and are cheaper to replace if lost or stolen. Tubes indeed have some good points: virtually no skill is required, they are easy to carry, are unsinkable, and on a hot day can be fun for a group. But in this author's opinion, the disadvantages of tubes outweigh any advantages. Since they cannot be controlled very well and are slow, tubes limit the extent of river that can be travelled in a given time. Beside this, they cannot carry anything, and worst of all their occupants must be partially submerged in the water. Even on warm days, dragging one's posterior in the river for hours can lead to a chill.

Rubber rafts are a somewhat better option than tubes. Rafts are ideal for beginners to go through rapids, or when the water is running high. Rafts can be maneuvered and can carry some amount of gear. However, rafts are cumbersome on the water, difficult to carry on land, and cannot make fast progress on the river.

Kayaks—the Eskimo and Aleut cousins of canoes—are sometimes seen on the Delaware. Kayaks come in two basic varieties: white water and cruising. White water kayaks are sleek one-occupant craft, ideally suited for playing the rapids at Skinners Falls, Mongaup Rift, and Wells Falls. White water kayaks, however, require considerable skill to manage in fast water. These craft cannot carry much baggage, and are ill-suited to the long slow sections of the Delaware. Cruising kayaks, including collapsibles, are built for one or two occupants. They can carry sufficient gear, and they work well in the Delaware's moderate rapids and slow pools. These kayaks are a specialty sort of boat, more often used for coastal adventures than inland rivers. A few outfitters offer both white water and cruising kayaks for use on the Delaware.

Canoes are definitely the craft of choice for the Delaware River. The highly maneuverable canoe is easy to carry and can make speedy forward progress, even loaded with all the gear needed for an extended trip. It offers a fine platform for fishing, but requires only elementary skill, and is relatively inexpensive. For general use on the Delaware, a plastic or composite (e.g., Royalex or Kevlar) canoe—the kind offered by most river outfitters—is preferred. A rockered high performance white-water canoe would not do well in the slow areas of the river; on the other hand, a keeled cruising canoe (designed for use on lakes) would be likely to hang up on the rocks in the rapids.

The Delaware River Watershed

The Delaware River begins at Hancock, New York, and flows 330.7 miles to the Atlantic Ocean at the mouth of Delaware Bay. Tides surge as far upstream as Trenton, 133 miles from the mouth. The

Delaware ranks seventeenth in length among the nation's rivers, draining 13,000 square miles, about one percent of the lower 48 states. Along the 197.5 miles above tidewater, the Delaware flows freely, unimpeded by artificial dams. There are three low wing dams constructed at natural rapids, but these do not significantly raise the level of the water behind them.

The slope of the river varies over its course, and generally drops less steeply (and consequently there are fewer rapids) the farther downstream one travels.

	ft./mi.
Hancock (mile 330, elev. 900 ft.)	
to Port Jervis (mile 254, elev. 420 ft.)	5.6
to Delaware Water Gap (mile 212, elev. 300 ft.)	2.8
to Trenton (mile 130, elev. 20 ft.)	3.4
TOTAL:	4.4

At the Milford, Pennsylvania, gauging station, the river flows at an average 2 1/2 million gallons per minute; at Trenton, 5 million gallons per minute.

There are four major tributaries to the Delaware above Trenton: the East and West Branches, the Neversink River, and the Lehigh River. Each is controlled by dams that impound water in great reservoirs for the use of the cities. There are several secondary tributaries—the Lackawaxen, Mongaup, Bushkill, Big Flatbrook, Paulinskill, Pequest, Musconetcong, and Assunpink—and scores of minor streams contributing to the flow of the Delaware.

The Delaware River typically runs high with snowmelt and April showers, but ebbs with the coming of summer. Less rain, increased evaporation, and reservoir draw-down often combine to produce extremely low flows by August. The Delaware swells somewhat in the autumn, then freezes over solidly by January.

Periodically the Delaware is subject to severe flooding, resulting in destruction of property and loss of life. A monster flood in 1841 destroyed almost all of the bridges that spanned the river at that time. Again in October 1903, the Delaware rose to destructive heights, forever remembered as the "Pumpkin Flood," for the hundreds of pumpkins that littered the riverbanks in the flood's wake. In August 1955, Hurricanes Connie and Diane combined to raise the Delaware to its greatest recorded height, causing scores of deaths and many millions of dollars of damage. Destructive floods have also been caused by snowmelt and sudden release of ice dams, most recently in January 1996; as of this writing, trees along the riverbanks have been scoured clean of their bark to a height of 20 feet by the 1996 flood.

River Conditions

The flow of the Delaware varies significantly with the seasons, weather, and releases from dams on the East and West Branches. Springtime typically provides high water; June, July, September, and October bring moderate water levels; in August, the river tends to be low. However, a dry spell can drop the river level in June, while a series of summer storms can bring floods in August (the greatest of all recorded floods on the Delaware occurred in August 1955).

The difficulty and duration of a canoe trip varies with the river level. The higher the river, the more difficult, but faster, the trip. When the river is low, plan on extra time to reach your destination.

Canoeists should always check the river conditions before embarking for a trip on the Delaware. On the upper river, the National Park Service maintains a "River Hotline" (914-252-7100) reporting river and weather conditions. River level is measured at an NPS gauging station at Narrowsburg. The NPS provides the following table of river levels:

Less than 2¹/₂ feet: Low water level—slow flow, many exposed rocks; may be necessary to carry or drag canoe in some areas.

2¹/₂ to 4 feet: Average water level—some exposed rocks in rapids, waves up to 3 feet; good level for boating.

4 to 6 feet: Moderately high water level—increased skills required, some rapids Class III; rafting recommended for less skilled boaters.

6 to 8 feet: High water level—high skill level required; rafting recommended for less experienced boaters. Not suited to open canoes.

8 to 12 feet: Very high water level—recommended only for highly skilled boaters in properly equipped rafts and/or closed boats.

12 to 17 feet: Approaching flood stage—boating is not recommended at this level!

Over 17 feet: Flood stage—boating not recommended!

River Rapids

This book uses the International Scale of River Difficulty to describe river rapids:

Class I—Moving water with a few riffles and small waves. Few or no obstructions.

Class II—Easy rapids with waves up to three feet and wide, clear channels that are obvious without scouting. Some maneuvering required.

Class III—Rapids with high, irregular waves capable of swamping an open canoe. Narrow passages that often require complex maneuvering. May require scouting from shore.

Class IV—Long, difficult rapids with constricted passages that require precise maneuvering in very turbulent waters. Scouting from shore necessary; conditions make rescue difficult. *Generally not possible for open canoes.* Boaters in covered canoes and kayaks should have the ability to Eskimo roll.

Class V—Extremely difficult, long, and very violent rapids with highly congested routes, which should always be scouted from shore. Rescue conditions difficult. Significant hazard to life in the event of a mishap. Ability to Eskimo roll essential for boaters in kayaks and decked canoes.

Class VI—Very dangerous, nearly impossible to navigate. For teams of experts only, after a close study has been made and all precautions taken.

There are no rapids on the Delaware River greater than Class III. Under normal conditions, only Wells Falls at Lambertville is rated above Class II. In moderately high water (4–6 feet), Skinners Falls, Shohola Rift, Foul Rift, and Wells Falls might all be considered Class III.

DRBC's 1964 maps classified Delaware River rapids on a scale from I to VI. However, this scale was unrelated to the International Scale of River Difficulty. Following the old DRBC maps, a canoeist might easily navigate a rapids marked as Class IV on the Delaware, only to believe mistakenly that he could paddle safely through a rapids marked as Class IV on another river. Until the 1979 DRBC maps corrected this problem, the standards for classification were entirely different.

The descriptions of rapids in this book are based on the moderate flow typical of late spring and early summer. Higher or lower flow might dramatically alter the characteristics of rapids, and this is noted to the extent possible. During the high cold flows of April, May, and early June, most Delaware rapids should be regarded as one class higher than indicated by this book and the DRBC maps. When flooding occurs, the river is too dangerous to canoe, regardless of the time of year.

The Delaware River in American History

Henry Hudson "discovered" the Delaware River in 1609, describing it as "one of the finest, best and pleasantest rivers in the world." Dutch colonists called the river the "South River" (the Hudson was the "North River"). The river is named for Thomas West, Baron De La Warr, governor of colonial Virginia from 1609 to 1618. Baron De La Warr was in residence at Jamestown for only two years, 1610 to 1611, and almost certainly never saw the river that was to bear his name.

The Delaware River has played an important role in American history, beginning with the communities of Indians and followed by the early settlements of Europeans along its valley, Washington's crossing of the Delaware during the Revolutionary War, and the growth of commerce and industrialization. Competition for use of the Delaware and desire for its control have ignited many controversies. Among these were the Walking Purchase of 1737, the Lackawaxen Crossing in 1829, the Tocks Island Dam in the 1960s and 1970s, the Point Pleasant diversion in the 1980s, and designation as a Wild and Scenic River in the present day.

In 1931 and 1954 the Supreme Court of the United States was called upon to apportion the water of the Delaware among the states whose boundaries are defined by the river. The Delaware River Basin Commission, made up of the governors of four states and the U.S. Secretary of the Interior, now oversees the use, development, and conservation of the river.

In 1764 Daniel Skinner tied a few logs together and floated them from Cochecton to market in Philadelphia; he was among the first to exploit the potential of the Delaware as a river of commerce. Later, "Durham boats"—shallow hulls 40, 50, and 60 feet long—shuttled merchandise among the growing villages on the Delaware. In these sturdy craft on Christmas night of 1776, George Washington and his freezing troops embarked to surprise

2. A timber raft bound for market. Crews of four to six raftsmen guided rafts like this from the Upper Delaware to Philadelphia. The 1904 version of the Mid-Delaware Bridge (Port Jervis-Matamoras) is in the background. Photo courtesy of the Pike County Historical Society.

the enemy at Trenton, an act that turned the tide of the American Revolution.

As America prospered, so did commerce on the Delaware. The Durham boats were replaced by canal barges toting coal, lumber, and iron in three major canals parallel to the river. Indeed, there are many people today who recall canalboats passing from Easton, through New Hope, Yardley, and Bristol with loads of coal for the furnaces of Philadelphia. But except for a few museum pieces, canal barges too have disappeared. Above tidewater, the Delaware has lost most of its value as an avenue of commerce.

Timber Rafting

Today rafting on the Delaware evokes the image of a few friends in an inflatable rubber raft, bobbing over rocks and through rapids. But in the last century rafting had an entirely different connotation. Huge log rafts up to 215 feet long were floated by the thousands every spring from the uppermost reaches of the Delaware down to Trenton and Philadelphia, their very structures comprised of timber for the market.

When the earliest pioneers settled the Upper Delaware Valley, their most formidable task was to clear the forest and make way for their little farm plots. Some of the timber was used to build houses, barns, and churches. More was saved for winter's fuel. But still these uses did not account nearly for the total timber that was felled. What was to be done with the excess?

The pioneers were nothing if not resourceful. With their immediate needs satisfied, they turned their attention to the booming growth of cities far downstream. In 1764, when Daniel Skinner of Cochecton bound his extra timber together, climbed on top, and floated two hundred miles to Philadelphia, the lumber-rafting industry of the Delaware was born.

Before long, farming had become merely a sideline for the valley people. Real prosperity was dependent on the annual timber sale. A typical farmer would harvest up to one hundred acres of woodland in the fall and winter. The logs were sledded and sluiced to piles near the river's edge. In early spring, hired hands made a raft by binding the logs with saplings, ropes, and iron spikes. At the first good flood, the raft, piled high with lumber, produce, or charcoal, was careering downstream to market.

The magnitude of the industry should not be underestimated. By 1828 at least 1,000 rafts a year passed Lackawaxen. Although the industry peaked in the 1850s, as late as 1875, 3,190 rafts were counted. In 1835 there were 208 sawmills in Sullivan County, New York, alone.

A trip down the Delaware by raft must have been an adventure. The rafts were sent during floods because the better clearance over rocks and obstructions and swift current made the trip much faster. Rafting from Callicoon to Trenton took only three and a half days in good conditions.

The rafts were made first of pine, then, as this resource was depleted, hemlock became the principal product. The logs and lumber were bound together by a transverse birch pole fastened by bent ashwood. In later days horseshoe-shaped iron spikes were used instead of ash. Huge oars were hung at the upstream and downstream ends, perfectly counterweighted for easy handling, to provide steering. In this way the raft could be moved side to side as it floated downstream. A typical raft was 120 feet long, 25 feet wide, and drew 2 feet of water. A raft builder, acting as steersman, would supervise four or six hired hands (often family) on the trip.

After making the trip year after year, many raftsmen became

known to one another. Some achieved the status of legend. Daniel Skinner, the "Lord Admiral of the Delaware," Depue Le Bar of Shawnee; Boney Quillen, the poet and chief jokester; and Deacon Mitchell, who raced from Hancock to Trenton in only two days, were among these.

The old dam at Lackawaxen, and numerous bridges with their narrow passages between piers, provided treacherous obstacles. But by far the most feared was Foul Rift. Many rafts were "stove-up" as they smashed the rocks in the mile-long rapid. Those who made it through were almost assured of a dowsing as the raft plunged over the final ledges.

Along the way, about a day's journey apart, certain places became popular stopping points. Hancock, at the confluence of the East and West Branches, and Tammany Flats, near Callicoon, were often jammed with rafters getting under way. At Big Eddy (Narrowsburg), rafts were sometimes so densely packed that a person could walk from one shore to the other by hopping from raft to raft. Dingmans Ferry was the next big way station, then Sandts Eddy just above Easton. Upper Black Eddy was most popular of all; it was a favorite carousing spot for raftsmen.

After delivering their rafts and cargo to market at Easton, Trenton, Bristol, or Philadelphia, the raftsmen had a long walk home but, with their satchels full of profit, it was a walk they didn't mind.

Scenic and Recreational River

By an act of the United States Congress (1978), 75 miles of the Delaware River, from Hancock to Sparrowbush (the Upper Delaware), and 40 miles from Milford, Pennsylvania, to the Delaware Water Gap (the Middle Delaware), were designated National Scenic and Recreational Rivers. Of course, the Upper Delaware has always been scenic and recreational, without the benefit of any act of Congress. But now, the law required that the river remain in that condition.

The river and adjacent lands of the Middle Delaware Scenic and Recreational River are within the Delaware Water Gap National Recreation Area. The National Park Service has completed a Management Plan for the Middle Delaware; enforcement of land use restrictions is straightforward, since the NPS owns and has jurisdiction over the land.

Management of the Upper Delaware Scenic and Recreational River, however, is another story. Virtually all lands adjacent to the river are privately owned, and regulated under state and local ordinances. The Park Service's early drafts of a management plan for the Upper Delaware were vehemently opposed by many local residents and governments, who feared that the Park Service would overregulate use of their property. Some even wanted Congress to rescind the Scenic and Recreational designation of the river.

In response to these concerns, the Park Service turned development of a management plan for the Upper Delaware over to the Conference of Upper Delaware Townships, representing the 15 New York and Pennsylvania municipalities that border the river from Hancock to Sparrowbush. The Conference, in cooperation with the states of New York and Pennsylvania, the Delaware River Basin Commission, the National Park Service, and a citizens' advisory board, completed the final River Management Plan in 1986. Implementation of the plan was then turned over to the Upper Delaware Council, a panel of 20 members including 16 representatives of local interests.

The emphasis in the Upper Delaware River Management Plan is on local control of land uses. The NPS would own only a few small parcels, including the Roebling Bridge at Lackawaxen and ranger offices, and would have no authority to regulate uses of private property adjacent to the river. The NPS role is to be essentially limited to management of recreation on the river itself, and representing the national interest as a member of the Upper Delaware Council.

Subject to action by the Upper Delaware Council and local authorities, the goals of the River Management Plan include:

1. Protect and maintain the scenic, cultural, and natural qualities of the Upper Delaware River corridor.
2. Conserve the resources of the Upper Delaware primarily through the use of existing local and state land-use controls and voluntary private landowner actions.
3. Protect private property rights, and allow for the use and enjoyment of the river corridor by both year-round and seasonal residents.
4. Provide for planned growth, while maintaining and conserving the essential character of the river valley.

3. National Park Service rangers, in canoes or skiffs, are a familiar sight on the Upper Delaware. Rangers provide law enforcement, visitor information, and safety services. Photo by the author.

5. Maintain and improve fisheries and wildlife habitat to ensure continued public enjoyment of hunting, fishing, and trapping.

6. Foster a public recognition of the Upper Delaware River Valley as a place with its own identity, continuing history, and a destiny to be shaped by its residents.

7. Provide for the continued public use and enjoyment of a full range of recreational activities.

8. Encourage maximum local government, private landowner, and citizen involvement in the management of the Upper Delaware.

On the river itself, however, the Park Service is boss. NPS rangers, in cooperation with state and local conservation officers and police, patrol the river throughout the year. The pale green NPS skiffs and canoes are a familiar sight along the way from Hancock to Port Jervis (indeed, all the way to the Delaware Water Gap). The NPS rangers, relieved from much of their traditional shore duties, can concentrate on making recreation on the Upper Delaware a safe and educational experience.

The National Park Service also sponsors numerous activities on the Upper Delaware, including visitor services, interpretive history and nature programs, canoe instruction and tours, and a "Volunteers in Parks" program in which citizens participate in rescue operations, canoe instruction, and information services.

Recently the NPS has set up a special phone number (914-252-7100) for river conditions. A taped message reports weather, water temperature, and river level, and provides advice for canoeists.

Water Quality

The United States Environmental Protection Agency considers all of the Delaware River from Hancock to Trenton to be suitable for the protection and propagation of fish, shellfish, and wildlife, and safe for recreation in and on the water. Indeed, water quality in the 120 miles from Hancock to the water gap is considered excellent, while from the water gap to Trenton the river is rated "good." In 1992, spurred by the Delaware Riverkeeper, the Delaware River Basin Commission adopted regulations classifying all of the river upstream from the Delaware Water Gap as "special protection waters" in which no degradation in water quality is permitted, even though the water quality already exceeds federal standards. The DRBC and National Park Service continue to seek a solution to nonpoint-source pollution, such as farm runoff, to even further improve water quality in the Delaware.

The Delaware was not always so clean. As long ago as 1799, a survey of the river near Philadelphia noted that the river was becoming contaminated by pollutants from ships, public sewers, and wharves. Over the years, the situation worsened. By 1940, aircraft pilots approaching Philadelphia were warned not to be alarmed by the stench of the Delaware River, detectable at 5,000 feet. The polluted waters corroded the hulls of ships. Even in the upstream areas, sewage discharges from Port Jervis, Stroudsburg, and Easton and the inflow of industrial wastes virtually killed segments of the Delaware. Raw sewage dumped into the river consumed most of the oxygen dissolved in the water, suffocating fish and other aquatic life. In the worst places, the river actually ran black and emitted the rotten-egg smell of hydrogen sulfide, a gas formed when organic material decays in the absence of oxygen.

By the late 1930s the Delaware River states could stand it no longer. A program to stem the pollution was launched for the length of the Delaware River. New laws in 1947 and 1972 established standards and required a special permit for any discharge of wastes into the river. Federal funds were granted for the construction of sewage treatment facilities. By the mid-1970s raw sewage was no longer being dumped into the Delaware River; nor did industry discharge noxious wastes there anymore. Use of the river as a sewer had ended.

Every year the river's water quality improves. The migration of shad, which had disappeared in the early part of the century, has returned and grows larger each year. The waters of the Delaware are clean, clear, and refreshing. Some local residents even complain that the river has become too clean, allowing for the propagation of troublesome insects, such as black flies, that were unknown when the water was more polluted.

This is not to say that there is no pollution in the Delaware River today. The treated effluent from village and city sewer systems is still discharged into its waters. Canoeists may notice these outfalls—usually along the length of a submerged pipe extending from the shore. A prominent example is the discharge from Easton, which is seen as a gray froth about a mile south of the city. This and other discharges, however, are rapidly absorbed and cleansed. Their effect on the river is negligible. Other pollutants enter the river from nonpoint sources, such as fertilizer runoff from fields, bacteria from livestock pens and pasturelands, and oily contaminants from roads and parking lots.

Although the Delaware River is clean enough for fishing and swimming, it is nowhere fit to drink. Microorganisms, such as Giardia and Crytosporidium, inhabit the river water. If ingested, these parasites can make a person quite sick for weeks. River water may be drunk if treated by boiling for at least a minute. Chemical disinfectants and water filters can reduce risk of contamination, but are probably not as effective as boiling. It is safest to drink water only from a known clean source—from home or a public water supply.

Canoe Safety

Drownings and near drownings are not uncommon on the Delaware River. And a drowning is eight times more likely in a

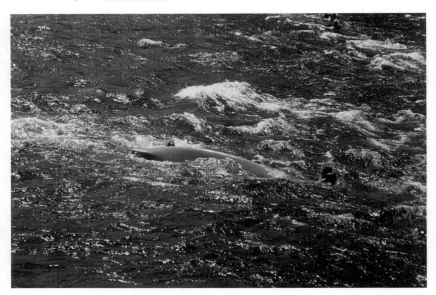

4. Capsize is common in the rapids on the Delaware. These dunked canoeists, at Mongaup Rift, would be safer at the upstream end of their canoe. Photo by the author.

canoeing accident than in any other type of boating mishap. At one time an average of 10 people per year drowned in the Delaware, although the average has declined since the National Park Service assumed jurisdiction over recreational uses of the upper reaches of the river. The NPS reports that there were 28 drownings on the Upper Delaware from 1980 to 1991. Most of these tragedies could have been avoided if only the canoeists had taken proper precautions or if they had not overestimated their abilities.

Most of the canoeists who paddle the Delaware River are novices, and for many, a trip on the Delaware is their very first canoeing experience. Unfortunately, many beginners do not want to admit to themselves or comrades that they are incapable of handling a canoe in all situations. Because of their pride, they do foolish things and take unnecessary chances. Novices should take a look at expert canoeists. Experts always wear personal floatation devices (PFDs) in white water, scout their routes before going through rapids, load their canoes properly, and are prepared for emergencies. Most experts have learned the hard way.

They know the experience of capsizing and being swept downstream by the overpowering flow of rapids. They know the effects of cold water and cold air. They have had to pull swamped canoes off rocks in a current. Many have had to rescue, or attempt to rescue, novices who did not know these things. Expert canoeists' pride has been washed away by close calls. They have learned to respect the river, and they are careful. Beginners must be even more careful.

Since drowning is the greatest danger in canoeing, the greatest single protection is the PFD, known to many as a life jacket. Federal regulations require that every boat, including canoes, have on board a PFD for each occupant. It is not required that the PFD be worn, but that it be available. It may not be necessary for good swimmers to wear a PFD when paddling in the numerous slow-moving stretches of the Delaware. But every canoeist should wear a PFD when approaching a rapid, in a heavy wind, or in unknown territory.

Even in slow-moving parts of the river, the current, unlike a swimmer, never tires. In a rapid, however, a person pitched into the water has no chance to overcome the current and can only hope to maneuver himself to safety. It is rare when at least one canoe in a party does not capsize in Skinners Falls, Mongaup Rift, Wells Falls, or many of the other rapids along the Delaware. When this happens, the canoeists are often saved only because they were wearing PFDs.

When a canoe does capsize or swamp in white water, its occupants must know what to do. First, they must get themselves upstream of the canoe. A canoe may appear light and maneuverable, but when filled with water, it becomes a one-ton mass capable of pinning and crushing a person against a rock. The capsized canoeist should make sure that his feet are pointed downstream to kick away from any obstructions that might be encountered. Until the shoreline or assistance is within reach, no attempt should be made to stand up in a rapid. A canoeist's feet can become wedged in a crevice or between rocks, with the current forcing the person face first into the water.

Because modern canoes don't sink, they provide additional flotation for capsized canoeists. Ten-foot-long ropes, called painters, may be tied to the bow and stern and dragged through the water, to be grabbed in the event of a capsize. There is no rapid in the Delaware River so long that it cannot be ridden out by a canoeist pitched from a canoe. Once in calmer waters, the canoeist can begin to collect him- or herself as well as the canoe, paddles, and remaining equipment and paraphernalia. Ideally, all loose gear should be securely tied into the canoe from the outset, in anticipation of such mishaps.

Novices should not attempt to canoe rapids that are beyond their ability. Beginners should avoid canoeing through Skinners Falls and Wells Falls by portaging around these rapids. In addition, the river segments between Narrowsburg and Port Jervis and between the water gap and Martins Creek are not suitable for beginners in canoes. No one should canoe after dark.

Another great danger to canoeists is hypothermia, or substantially reduced body temperature. Hypothermia, which can be fatal, causes disorientation, lack of coordination, and drowsiness. It is a more serious threat in the spring and fall months when the water and air are cool, but extended exposure in the summer can also cause hypothermia. A person capsized into water below 55° Fahrenheit may be in trouble. The body loses heat 40 times faster in water than in air; under such circumstances hypothermia can begin to take effect in a matter of minutes. The best prevention is staying out of cold water. In the spring the Delaware River runs higher as well as colder, and the rapids are more difficult than during the typically moderate summer flows. Under these conditions canoeing the white water stretches should be attempted only by the experienced, who should dress warmly (even in wetsuits), bring extra dry clothes, travel in groups, and wear PFDs.

Cuts and scrapes are another hazard. A capsize in a rapid often results in assorted abrasions. Even in slow-moving sections of the river, swimmers frequently strike subsurface rocks. Canoeists should wear sneakers or moccasins at all times (preferably an old pair with holes along the bottom so water can run out). Swimming should be attempted only in areas known to be safe and free of hazards.

Sunburn is probably the most frequent injury suffered on the river. Canoeists, especially beginners, often think that a day on the river is a great time to work on their tans—and so go home with severe, blistering sunburns. There is no shade on the river, and the sun blazes down all day long. Reflection off the water makes matters worse. On sunny days an aluminum canoe becomes an oven that will slowly bake its unprotected occupants. For protection against sunburn, bring plenty of lotion, especially for the shoulders and thighs. Wear a hat, and keep a long-sleeved shirt and long trousers handy.

In addition, there are numerous minor hazards that may be encountered. The river islands teem with mosquitoes and yellow jackets. Poison ivy and stinging nettles are thick on the islands and along the riverbanks. Some sections of the river are popular with motorboaters and Jet Skiers; in these areas canoeists should stay near the shoreline. Although awareness and avoidance of these hazards is the best prevention, every party of canoeists should carry at least one well-stocked first-aid kit.

A safe canoe trip makes for a good canoe trip. By taking precautions, using common sense, and staying within the limits of their ability, canoeists on the Delaware River can be assured of a fun-filled and rewarding experience.

Canoe Trip Checklist

One of the advantages of a canoe is that sufficient gear can be brought along, whether for a one-day outing or two-week excursion. Of course, it is easiest to travel light, but there are some essentials that should always be carried on any canoe trip. The following are "musts" for every canoe trip, no matter how long.

1. Personal Flotation Device (PFD, or life jacket); it is required by law that a PFD be carried for each occupant of every canoe.
2. Extra paddle, securely lashed to the canoe, to be used as a replacement when your primary paddles get washed away.
3. A bailer (cut the bottom out of an empty one-gallon bleach bottle, then use the top part—with the handle—to bail), and a large sponge.
4. Extra dry clothes, in a watertight bag or container, to change into when the day is done.
5. Sun protection, including lotion, hat, and sunglasses.
6. Fresh water—plan to drink plenty each day on the river.
7. Garbage bags. Leave no trash in or on the river!
8. Insect repellent.
9. First-aid kit, including items to treat injuries likely to be

encountered: cuts and scrapes, insect bites and stings, sore muscles, sunburn.

10. Rope and/or bungee cords to secure gear into the canoe.

Remaining gear to be carried depends on the length of the trip, the weather, accommodations if overnight, what and where the canoeists will be eating, personal interests (wildlife? photography? fishing?), and preferences.

The Delaware Riverkeeper

Inspired by Hudson Riverkeeper John Cronin, in 1988 Cynthia Poten founded the Delaware Riverkeeper network, a citizens' action group for the river and watershed. The Riverkeeper is headquartered in historic Washington Crossing, Pennsylvania, with offices in Narrowsburg, New York, and Camden, New Jersey. The Riverkeeper coordinates the efforts of hundreds of volunteers who test water quality at 75 monitoring points throughout the watershed; advise public agencies such as DRBC, the National Park Service, and state and local governments; and spot water and land-use problems that could adversely affect the river. The Riverkeeper campaigns for conservation of the land and water throughout the Delaware watershed. Among other victories, the Riverkeeper has gained special protection status for water quality in the Upper Delaware, prevented the introduction of Pacific salmonid species into the watershed, and advocated the limitation of new exports of Delaware River water. On the community awareness front, the Riverkeeper sponsors field trips and special group canoe trips, participates in arts festivals and other community events, and is a sponsor of the Delaware River Sojourn, an annual river trip down selected portions of the Delaware.

Today the Riverkeeper Network is funded by grant awards, private contributions, and citizen lawsuits against polluters under the state and federal laws. To raise public awareness, the Riverkeeper recently began selling "shares in the Delaware" at $1.00 per share; each "share" is represented by a colorful print of a fish indigenous to the river. Dividends are paid in cleaner water and healthier habitat.

For information about the Riverkeeper Network, or to report incidents of pollution or other improper river uses, the Delaware Riverkeeper can be contacted at P.O. Box 356, Washington

Crossing, Pennsylvania 18977-0326, 215-369-1188 or 800-8-DELAWARE.

Fishing the Delaware River

While this is not a book about fishing, no guide to the Delaware could be complete without acknowledging the thousands of anglers who try their skill—and luck—on the river. And more often than not, they are rewarded for their efforts with a string of bass, a pan of trout, or perhaps a trophy muskellunge. The clean, cool water of the Delaware is a perfect home for many species of game fish.

A valid license (and special stamp if fishing for trout) is required to fish anywhere on the Delaware. When fishing from the riverbank, anglers must have a license issued by that state; when fishing from a canoe or other boat, they may have a license issued by either state (New York or Pennsylvania north of Port Jervis; New Jersey or Pennsylvania south of Port Jervis). During designated "fish for free" days each June a license is not required, although all other regulations apply. The National Park Service and state fish and game authorities patrol the river and regularly check for fishing licenses; a costly summons will be issued to persons fishing without one, and the property of violators may be confiscated. Licenses may be purchased at most sporting goods stores throughout the Delaware Valley, or through the state fish and game authorities.

Neither anglers nor canoeists have the right-of-way on the river. Sometimes, however, one or the other behave as if they do, and ugly confrontations have been known to occur. Canoeists must take care not to interfere with people fishing; common sense and courtesy will usually make for a pleasant day on the river for all. When approaching anglers, keep as much distance as possible (hopefully, the fisherman won't be standing in the only canoeable passage); if the angler is in the middle, it is usually best to pass behind him or her. Check to see where the angler's line is, and be sure to avoid canoeing across it. When in doubt, don't hesitate to ask. Be quiet to avoid scaring the fish or (more likely) making the anglers think you are scaring the fish. There are certain times and places where fishing reigns, and it may be best to canoe another day. The opening weekends of trout season on the Upper Delaware, or during one of the many shad tournaments in spring, would not be the best days for a canoe trip.

The best times and places to catch the various species of game fish on the Delaware—and any special regulations that may apply—can be found by contacting state fish and game authorities. There are several good books detailing the habits of the fish, bait or lures to use, and techniques for fishing success on the Delaware. Some are listed in the bibliography of this book, and still others may be found in NPS and local bookstores. The following is a summary of the major species of game fish that may be caught in the Delaware River.

Trout: The Delaware River from Hancock to Callicoon is one of the finest trout streams in the east. Both brown trout (to 17 inches, 1 1/2 lb.) and rainbow trout (to 16 inches, 2 lbs.) are abundant and regularly caught. The best fishing is late May and early June. Limits: the first Saturday after April 11 to September 30, 14-inch minimum, limit one fish per day.

Shad: These robust fish (typically 15 inches, 7 lbs.) migrate each spring from the sea to their spawning grounds in the Delaware. As the schools move up the river, shad can be caught in abundance; many communities have annual tournaments to catch trophy shad. Limits: All year, any size, daily limit of six fish.

Bass: Probably the most reliable of Delaware River game fish, both smallmouth (most common, to 24 inches, 5 lbs.) and largemouth (to 26 inches, 10 lbs.) bass can be caught the entire length of the river. Limits: All year, 12-inch minimum, daily limit of five.

Striped bass: Thanks to improvement in water quality, fishing for striped bass (known in some areas as rockfish) gets better every year. Large spawning stripers (to 30 inches, 10 lbs.) ascend and descend the river during June and October, and can be caught in the deeper pools; all through the summer and fall the river is a nursery for small (to 14 inches) stripers. Limits: All year, 28-inch minimum, daily limit two fish.

Walleye: Bottom feeders, walleye (average 18 inches, about 4 lbs.) are found in the deep holes throughout the river; the best fishing is on spring nights. Limits: Season begins first Saturday in May; 18-inch minimum, daily limit three fish.

Pickerel: These slender fighters (20 to 30 inches, 5 to 10 lbs.)

are found in weedy shallows and eddies, especially in the upper reaches of the river. Limits: All year, 12-inch minimum, daily limit five fish.

Muskellunge: The Pennsylvania Fish Commission stocked a few muskies near the Delaware Water Gap in the early 1970s, and a healthy population of these monsters (up to 50 inches, 40 lbs.) now thrives in the river. Limits: All year, 30-inch minimum, daily limit two fish.

Eel: Every summer, during dark nights, these snakelike fish (to 48 inches, 2 lbs.) migrate from their home territory on the Upper Delaware to the Sargasso Sea in the mid-Atlantic to spawn. This is the only species fished commercially on the Delaware; the V-shaped eel weirs are common obstacles to canoeists on the Upper Delaware. Limits: All year, any size, no limit.

Panfish: Sunfish, bluegills and fallfish (to about 12 inches) are abundant throughout the Delaware. They are easily caught, even by novices. Limits: All year, any size, no limit.

Carp, catfish, suckers: These bottom feeders can be found throughout the river, especially in slow-moving and muddy water. Delaware River carp can be huge (to 48 inches). Limits: All year, any size, no limit.

Hancock to Kellams Bridge

Mile 330.7 to 312.6 (18.1 miles, plus 4.6 miles from Balls Eddy access area)

The Delaware River begins just below Hancock, New York, at the confluence of the East and West Branches. At this uppermost part, the Delaware River is its shallowest and also most narrow. There are no major rapids, and only a few riffles rated Class I. Except for the peak of trout season, river traffic tends to be light.

The river flows through the Appalachian Plateau's geophysical province, which is composed predominantly of shale and sandstone rock extending in a broad band from northern New York to northern Alabama. The foothills of New York's Catskill Mountains lie to the north of the river, and the northern Pocono Mountains of Pennsylvania are to the south. The region was covered by glaciers within the last 20,000 years.

Today the banks of the Delaware and nearby hills are almost entirely clothed in hardwood forest. But in the nineteenth century, most of the trees were stripped from the hills and floated downstream to the markets in the big cities.

Many varieties of waterfowl make their home on and near the river, and small game animals abound in the woods nearby. Deer are frequently seen near the water's edge, and beaver are common in the river. Black bear are not uncommon in the forests. This section of the Delaware, famous for trout fishing, is very popular with anglers in the spring.

Flow in the East and West Branches is controlled by the Pepacton and Cannonsville reservoirs, respectively. Until the mid-1970s, there was little effort to control releases from these reservoirs with respect to effects on the mainstream Delaware. As a result, this section of the Delaware River often ran extremely low in the summertime, sometimes so low that canoes had to be dragged over shallow areas. The nearly stagnant water became so warm that trout and other cold-water fish could not survive. The Delaware River Basin Commission now manages reservoir releases to maintain fish populations, and there is always enough flow for canoes.

There are three public access areas in this section of the Delaware, plus two more not far up the West Branch. There is no authorized public access at the end of this section.

Balls Eddy, Pennsylvania, Mile 4.6, West Branch
Shehawken, Pennsylvania, Mile 0.6, West Branch
Buckingham, Pennsylvania, Mile 325.1
Lordville, New York, Mile 321.6
Long Eddy, New York, Mile 315.5.

Most land adjacent to the river are privately owned, and trespassers are not welcome. The National Park Service and local law authorities will ticket or arrest trespassers. Camping is allowed only at private campgrounds.

This entire section is within the Upper Delaware National Scenic and Recreational River, and recreation on the river is under the jurisdiction of the National Park Service. Call 914-252-7100 for river conditions.

River Guide

Map 1

Mile 4.6, West Branch. Balls Eddy access area, provided by the Pennsylvania Fish Commission. Parking, boat ramp, trash disposal, privies. Access from Pennsylvania Route 191. All boats, including canoes, launched or landed at Pennsylvania Fish Commission access areas, must bear a valid Pennsylvania boat registration.

0.6, West Branch. Shehawken access area, provided by the Pennsylvania Fish Commission, at the mouth of Shehawken Creek. Very limited parking, natural launch area, no facilities. Access from Pennsylvania Route 191, at junction of Pennsylvania Route 370. All boats must bear a valid Pennsylvania boat registration.

Mile 330.7. The Delaware River begins at the confluence of the East and West Branches, which flow from the Catskill Mountains. The East Branch was formerly known as the Popaxtunk, and the West Branch the Mohawks Branch.

The community of Hancock, New York, is one mile upstream on the East Branch.

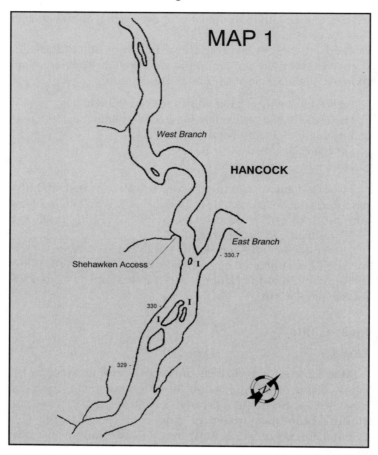

Point Mountain, elevation 1,380 feet, rises between the East and West Branches just above their confluence.

This is the upstream boundary of the Upper Delaware National Scenic and Recreational River. From this point 78 miles to Sparrowbush, recreation on the river is under the jurisdiction of the National Park Service.

A spit of marshy land extends downstream about 100 yards on the Pennsylvania side. There is a Class I rapids near the spit.

330.3. City of Hancock water treatment plant, New York side.

330.0. Upstream end of a low island. Channels to the left and right are passable. Sinuous channels lead through the island from the right channel. There is a Class I rapids in both left and right channels.

329.7. Downstream end of island; a second island begins. There is a Class I rapids in the channel between the islands. Right channel is quite shallow.

329.3. Downstream end of island.

329.0. Shingle Hollow Brook, Pennsylvania side.

328.7. French Woods Creek enters, New York side.

328.6. McCoys Knob, elevation 1,800 feet, rises steeply on the New York side.

328.0. River bends widely to the right.

327.7. A shallow rock ledge extends diagonally upstream from the New York side provides a Class I rapids. Extreme left end of ledge may be hazardous at low water level.

327.3. Stockport Creek enters, Pennsylvania side.

Map 2

326.6. Low grassy gravel island on left. There are mild riffles in the channels both left and right of the island.

River bends sharply left.

326.4. River bends back to the right; Class I rapids—beware submerged rocks; grassy gravel bar on the left side of the river.

326.1. Blue Mill Stream, New York side, under a stone-arch culvert.

325.9. River bends sharply right; very shallow or exposed gravel bar on left. A Class I rapids without obstructions; standing waves to 1¹/₂ feet.

325.2. Nabbys Brook enters, Pennsylvania side.

325.0. Buckingham access area, Pennsylvania, maintained by the Pennsylvania Fish Commission. Parking, rough stone boat ramp, trash disposal, privies. Access from Pennsylvania Route 191. All boats must bear a valid Pennsylvania boat registration.

324.8. Class I rapids.

323.7. Upstream end of Frisbie Island, extending .6 mile downstream. Channels to the left and right are passable though shallow. There are Class I rapids without obstruction in the left channel near the upstream end of the island.

323.1. Downstream end of Frisbie Island, with shallows and gravel bars extending a short distance downstream. The channels near the Pennsylvania side and between the gravel bars present Class I rapids.

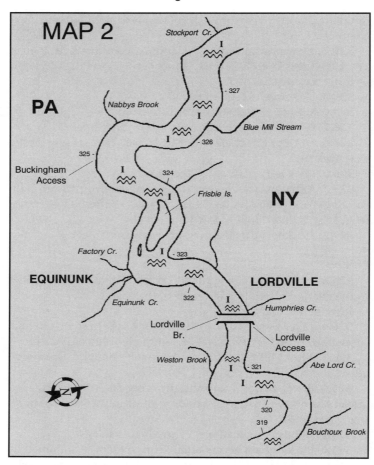

MAP 2

Stockport Cr.

PA

Nabbys Brook

327

Blue Mill Stream

326

325

Buckingham
Access

324

Frisbie Is.

NY

Factory Cr.

323

EQUINUNK

LORDVILLE

Equinunk Cr.

322

Humphries Cr.

Lordville
Br.

Lordville
Access

Weston Brook

321

Abe Lord Cr.

320

319

Bouchoux Brook

322.6. Factory Creek enters, Pennsylvania side, with gravel bars extending into the river.

The community of Equinunk, Pennsylvania, is on the right; limited services. There is no access to or from the river.

322.5. Equinunk Creek enters, Pennsylvania side.

322.4. Rocky cliffs on the Pennsylvania side.

321.7. A Class I rapids without obstructions.

321.6. Humphries Creek enters, New York side.

Pass under the Lordville Bridge, constructed in 1992. A bridge constructed at this site in 1869 was destroyed in the flood of 1903. A one-lane suspension bridge built in 1904 was demolished in 1988. A gauge painted on the center pier of the bridge measures the river level.

Lordville access area, New York, provided by the New York Department of Environmental Conservation, located under the Lordville Bridge. Very limited parking, rough launch area, no facilities.

The hamlet of Lordville, New York, is on the left. No services.

321.0. Abe Lord Creek enters, New York side, at a constriction of the river.

Class I rapids with submerged and protruding boulders, New York side.

320.8. Weston Brook enters, Pennsylvania side.

320.1. Shallows or exposed gravel bars on the Pennsylvania side. A Class I rapid without obstructions.

319.7. River bends sharply left; steep wooded slopes on the Pennsylvania side.

319.0. Bouchoux Brook, New York side, via an arched culvert under the Erie Railroad.

318.8. River bends sharply right. Pennsylvania side is quite shallow.

Map 3

318.7. Snow Creek enters, cascading several hundred feet from cliffs on the New York side

318.6. Class I rapids.

The lands on the New York side are within a State Forest Preserve, continuing about one mile downstream. There is no access from the river.

Jensen Hill rises steeply on the New York side.

318.4. River broadens and becomes very shallow. Gravel may be exposed on the right and left center.

317.2. River continues very shallow on right; grassy gravel islands in the river are submerged when the river level is moderately high.

Class I rapids around exposed or submerged boulders to the left of the islands.

315.7. Pea Brook enters, New York side. River narrows considerably to the right as gravel deposits encroach on the left.

315.6. Hoolihan Brook enters, New York side. Gravel bar at mouth of stream extends into the river.

315.5. Long Eddy access area, New York, maintained by the

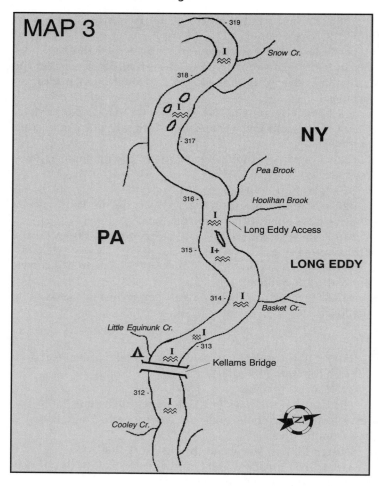

MAP 3

- 319

Snow Cr.

I
〰〰

318 -

317

NY

Pea Brook

316 -

Hoolihan Brook

PA

I
〰〰

Long Eddy Access

315 -   I+
〰〰

LONG EDDY

314 -   I
〰〰

Basket Cr.

Little Equinunk Cr.

I
〰〰

- 313

Kellams Bridge

312 -

I
〰〰

Cooley Cr.

village of Long Eddy. Rough launch area, no parking, no facilities. Access from New York Route 97.

The community of Long Eddy, New York, is on the left. Limited services.

Enter a Class I rapids; no obstructions.

315.0. A low gravel island on the New York side. The left channel is very shallow at low water.

There is a Class I+ rapids between the Pennsylvania side and the island—watch for submerged boulders.

5. Great blue herons are abundant on the Delaware River. Photo by Courtenay Kling.

314.9. Downstream end of island. Shallows or exposed gravel in the right channel; standing waves to 1½ feet on the right.

314.7. Old stone bridge abutment, Pennsylvania side.

314.1. Basket Creek enters, New York side. Extensive gravel bar at mouth of creek extends to middle of river and downstream. New York Route 97 crosses Basket Creek on a high concrete bridge.

313.9. Class I rapids around gravel bars—very shallow.

313.4. Class I rapids with no obstructions.

312.7. Little Equinunk Creek enters, Pennsylvania side. There is a Class I rapids between the gravel bars at the mouth of the creek and the New York side.

Camping. Soaring Eagle Campground. Tent sites near the river, all facilities. R.D. 1, Box 300, Equinunk, Pennsylvania 18417, 717-224-4666.

312.6. Pass under the Kellams-Stalker Bridge. Completed in 1890, this is the third-oldest existing span across the Delaware. The suspension cables hang below the one-lane road surface in the center.

Kellams Bridge to Narrowsburg

Mile 312.6 to 289.9 (22.7 miles)

With the inflow of numerous small streams, the flow of the Delaware is slightly greater than in the preceding section, although for the most part the river remains shallow and narrow. The highlight of this section is famous Skinners Falls, a severe Class II rapid at Mile 295.2. This section is renowned for fishing, and canoeists must take special care to avoid interfering with anglers. Canoe traffic is relatively light above Skinners Falls, but below that point can sometimes resemble a Los Angeles freeway.

Callicoon and Narrowsburg, New York, are the principal towns along this section, although services can also be found in several places along New York Route 97, which is close to the river most of the way. Secondary roads approach the river on the Pennsylvania side at Callicoon and between Damascus and Narrowsburg. The Erie Railroad runs very close to the river on the New York riverbank.

The river continues to flow through the Appalachian Plateau's geophysical province. There are several locations of exposed bedrock, the most prominent at Skinners Falls. The banks of the river are almost entirely forested, although in a few areas fields have been cleared for farming. Water birds are especially abundant here. Numerous bald eagles make their winter home in the nearby hills, and a few are known to nest in the area.

Eel traps, or weirs, are encountered in several places downstream from Kellams, continuing to the Delaware Water Gap. Eels are fish that resemble three-foot snakes. They are "catadromous," i.e., resident in the fresh water of the Upper Delaware and migrating every autumn to spawn in the sea. For unknown reasons, they travel only on moonless nights. Eel weirs are constructed of two low stone walls, 50 feet or more in length, which meet at the point of a downstream "V." The migrating eels get funneled to the point of the "V," where they are trapped in a grate from

6. A volunteer of the National Canoe Safety patrol (in kayak) keeps a watchful eye on a scout troop passing through Skinners Falls. Photo by Courtenay Kling.

which they are raked into sacks. Not many Americans appreciate the flavor of eels, so most of the harvest is exported to Europe, where eel is considered a delicacy.

In the years when timber rafting was a major industry on the Delaware River, eel weirs were considered an obstruction and were outlawed. Canoeists today must remember that eel weirs are private property, constructed and used under a permit from fish and game authorities. Canoeists should pass in the channel to the left or right of the weir wings, or through the center chute if no trap is present; don't go over the rock wings

There is no authorized public access at the beginning of this section of the river. Six public access areas are available along the way:

Callicoon, New York, Mile 303.6
Callicoon, Pennsylvania, Mile 303.1
Damascus, Pennsylvania, Mile 298.3
Skinners Falls, New York, Mile 295.4

7. An eel weir near Port Jervis. Eels are trapped in the apex of the weir during their migration to the sea. Photo by the author.

Narrowsburg, New York, Mile 290.1
Narrowsburg, Pennsylvania, Mile 289.9.

Virtually all of the lands adjacent to the river are privately owned, and trespassers are not welcome. Camping is allowed only at private campgrounds.

The river here is designated as a National Scenic and Recreational River, and recreation on the river is under the jurisdiction of the National Park Service. Call 914-252-7100 for the NPS report of river conditions.

River Guide

Map 4

312.6. Pass under the Kellams-Stalker Bridge. Constructed in 1890, this is the third-oldest extant span across the Delaware. The suspension cables hang below the one-lane road surface in the center.

311.5. Cooley Creek enters from a marshy area on the Pennsylvania side.

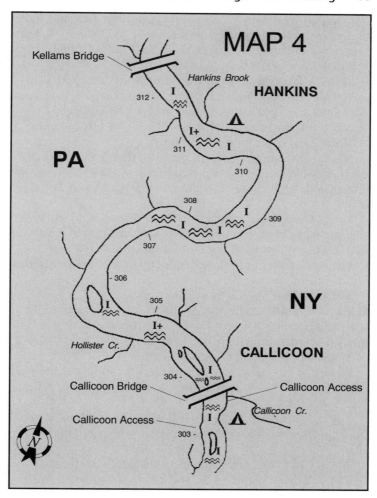

Enter a Class I+ rapids—no obstructions, but big waves.

310.9. Hankins Brook enters, New York side. Gravel deposits at the mouth of the creek narrow the river considerably, creating an exciting Class I+ rapids with standing waves to 2½ feet.

310.8. Class I rapid continues over submerged boulders. Very shallow on the left.

The community of Hankins, New York, founded in 1834, is on the left. Limited services.

Camping. Red Barn Campground: riverfront tent and trailer sites, showers, laundry, camp store. May 1 to October 15, reservations recommended. Hankins, New York 12741 914-887-4995.

310.0. River bends sharply to the right.

309.4. A small creek enters through culvert, New York side.

308.5. River continues right turn. A Class I rapids, with boulders and submerged ledges, is near the New York side.

308.1. A Class I rapids extending .3 mile; no obstructions.

307.9. Slow water for next 2 miles.

305.8. Upstream end of large vegetated island. The right channel is passable, but boulders protrude at low water. Main current flows through left channel. There are large boulders near the left bank.

305.5. Downstream end of island. A Class I rapid in the left channel without obstructions. There is a small gravel bar in the middle of the channel at the downstream end of the island.

The clock tower of St. Joseph's Seminary at Callicoon stands on the hillside ahead.

305.1. Hollister Creek enters, Pennsylvania side. A gravel bar at the mouth of the creek extends halfway across the river. There is a Class I+ rapids between the bar and the New York side. Submerged boulders on left may be hazardous.

304.4. Upstream end of a grassy island.

A trace of an old eel weir lies in the left channel at the head of the island. The left channel is passable to the right of the eel weir, but shallow.

The right channel, though narrower, is deeper. A small gravel island in the right channel begins just below the head of the main island.

304.3. Class I rapids in channel to the left of the island.

304.0. Gravel island ends, and another begins. There is a Class I rapid over the shallows between the islands and along the Pennsylvania side.

303.7. Pass under the concrete Callicoon Bridge, constructed in 1961. There is a short Class I rapid immediately under the bridge.

Landers River Trips base, New York side, immediately past the bridge; this is not a public access.

Callicoon Creek enters, New York side. A wide gravel bar at the mouth of the creek extends halfway across the river.

8. Main Street, Callicoon, New York. Most of the buildings in Callicoon were erected shortly after the town was devastated by fire and flood in 1888. Photo by the author.

303.6. Callicoon access area, New York, maintained by the New York Department of Environmental Conservation. There is ample parking, natural boat launch, trash disposal, and privies. Access at south end of Main Street.

The community of Callicoon, New York, is accessible from the access area. Callicoon began as a center of timber rafting, and grew with arrival of the Erie Railroad in the 1840s. Many of the buildings in the downtown area were constructed in 1888, after the town was devastated by fire.

Lunch: Callicoon advertises itself as the "dining capital of Sullivan County"; there are numerous eating places, from cafes to fine gourmet restaurants.

303.5. Camping. Upper Delaware Campgrounds, a full service campground on the river's edge. There are about 225 sites, modern sanitary facilities with showers, a swimming pool, ice, firewood, and a camp store. Box 331, Callicoon, New York 12723, 914-887-5344/5110.

Map 5

303.1. Callicoon access area, Pennsylvania, maintained by the Pennsylvania Fish Commission. Along with ample parking, there are a natural launch area, trash disposal, and privies. Access from State Road 1016. All boats must bear a valid Pennsylvania registration.

303.0. Upstream end of a low gravel island, submerged at moderately high water. Channels left and right of the island are passable with Class I rapids.

302.9. Downstream end of gravel island. Another small gravel bar and shallows in the middle of the river, submerged at high water level.

302.8. Enter Bush's Eddy, slow water for the next mile. The lands along the New York side were once known as St. Tammany Flats, a starting place for many timber rafts.

Look back upriver for a good view of Callicoon and St. Joseph's Seminary.

301.9. A small creek enters from a marsh, Pennsylvania side. In the river, there is a Class I rapid with no obstructions

301.2. Downstream end of Big Island, a grassy marsh on the left. The left channel is dry at the upstream end of the "island."

300.3. Upstream end of a low vegetated gravel island. The left channel is very shallow and may be blocked by gravel bars at very low water. There is an old eel weir in the right channel at the head of the island, making a Class I rapids.

300.0. Tapered downstream end of gravel island. There is another small island nestled near the New York side. Class I rapids over shallows without obstructions.

299.9. River bends sharply to the right.

The old Cochecton cemetery is situated on the New York riverbank.

299.2. Schoolhouse Creek enters, Pennsylvania side.

299.1. A Class I rapid without obstructions.

298.8. River bends back to the left.

298.5. Abutment of old Damascus bridge, Pennsylvania side. Cribs for piers of the old bridge can be seen on the river bottom.

Power lines cross the river.

298.4. Pass under the steel-truss Cochecton-Damascus Bridge, built in 1952. The communities of Cochecton, New York, and Damascus, Pennsylvania, are at opposite ends of the bridge.

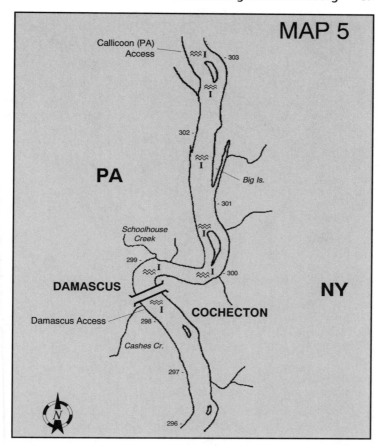

MAP 5

Callicoon (PA) Access

303

302

PA

Big Is.

301

Schoolhouse Creek

299

300

DAMASCUS

NY

Damascus Access

298

COCHECTON

Cashes Cr.

297

296

298.3. Damascus access area, Pennsylvania, maintained by the Pennsylvania Fish Commission. Parking, boat ramp, trash disposal, telephone, privies. Access from Pennsylvania Route 371. All boats must bear a valid Pennsylvania registration.

Cashes Creek (also known as Beaverdam Creek) enters, Pennsylvania side, at the access area.

297.8. A low vegetated gravel bar in the middle of the river; submerged at moderately high water. Left channel is narrow and shallow but passable.

Fast water and riffles over shallows, next .4 mile.

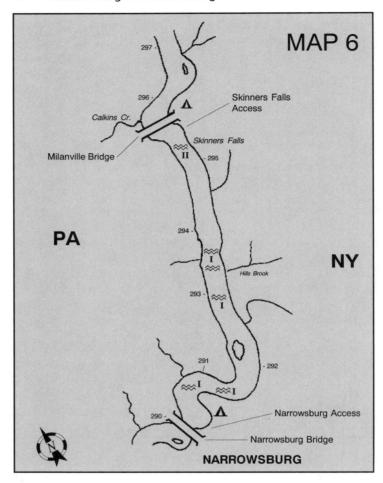

Map 6

296.7. Mitchell Pond Brook enters, New York side.

296.5. A brushy island on left; the narrow channel to the left of the island is navigable and makes an interesting side trip.

River bends to the right.

295.6. Calkins Creek enters, Pennsylvania side.

295.4. Camping. Landers River Trips has a canoe base and campground just upstream from the Milanville-Skinners Falls Bridge. There are riverfront tent sites and lean-tos, camp store,

9. A sign on the Milanville–Skinners Falls Bridge warns of the hazards waiting around the next bend. Photo by the author.

and hot showers. Landers River Trips, 1336 New York Route 97, Narrowsburg, New York 12764, 914-252-3925 / 800-252-3925.

Pass under the Milanville-Skinners Falls Bridge. Built in 1901, this steel-truss span has a wood-plank road surface. A sign on the center pier of the bridge warns of the rapids ahead.

The hamlet of Milanville, Pennsylvania, is on the right.

National Park Service ranger offices (North District) are located 1/4 mile up the road from the Pennsylvania end of the bridge.

Skinners Falls access area, New York, maintained by the New York Department of Environmental Conservation, just downstream from the bridge. There is ample parking, a natural boat launch area, trash disposal, and privies. The National Park Service maintains an information kiosk here. Access from Milanville Road, off New York Route 97.

295.3. Entrance Rock, a big square boulder on the left, signals the approach to Skinners Falls. A buoy advises "WARNING—rapids ahead—wear your life jacket."

295.2. Enter Skinners Falls, a Class II rapids, one of the most severe on the Delaware River. Before the National Park Service

10. Exposed shale ledges and swift current make for treacherous going at Skinners Falls. The Milanville–Skinners Falls Bridge, constructed in 1901, is in the background. Photo by the author.

11. The water-worn shale ledges at Skinners Falls. In some places potholes several feet deep have been gouged into the rock by the turbulent flow. Photo by Courtenay Kling.

12. Bird's-eye view of Skinners Falls. In one of the most hazardous rapids on the Delaware, the river plunges over a series of ledges. Photo courtesy of Stuart Gillard.

gained jurisdiction over recreation on the river, there were frequent drownings at Skinners Falls. Now, on summer weekends, members of the National Canoe Safety Patrol volunteer as "lifeguards," and while many boaters still upset in Skinners Falls, drownings rarely occur.

The main channel through Skinners Falls flows along the Pennsylvania side. A series of rock ledges guards the New York side. However, the character of and routes through Skinners Falls change dramatically with the water level; canoeists should always scout the route before going though. Wear PFDs! Novices should consider running Skinners Falls in a raft, or portaging canoes.

295.1. Skinners Falls ends. River is slow for next 2 miles.

294.1. There is an old eel weir in the left center of the river. Passage is clear on both sides.

293.7. River narrows at a broad gravel bar on the right. There are two low gravel bars in the main channel, submerged at moderately high water, and Class I rapids on both sides. An old eel weir, left side of the river, can be passed over at moderate water level. Rocks on the left may be a hazard.

293.1. Hills Brook enters, New York side.

293.0. Eel weir, in use in 1996, in the middle of the river. Passage around the weir on the left and right presents Class I rapids.

292.1. A low grassy gravel bar, middle of the river. Passage is clear and current swift in left and right channels.

291.6. River bends sharply right.

291.3. A Class I rapids over ledges extending across the river. Main channel is in right center with standing waves to 1½ feet.

291.0. Riffles continue over ledges.

290.9. An unnamed stream enters, Pennsylvania side, at a marshy area.

290.5. River bends sharply left and becomes quite narrow.

Pass under power lines marked by red balls.

290.2. Camping. Landers River Trips campground and canoe base, New York side: riverfront tent sites and lean-tos, all services. Landers River Trips, 1336 New York Route 97, Narrowsburg, New York 12764 914-252-3925 / 800-252-3925.

290.1. Narrowsburg access area, New York, maintained by New York Department of Environmental Conservation. There is ample parking, a paved boat ramp, trash disposal, and privies. From the river, look for the log bulkhead. Access from DeMauro Lane in Narrowsburg (by Tusten Town Hall and Theatre), off Sullivan County Route 24.

River bends sharply right, constricting into a narrow passage between rocky ledges.

290.0. Pass under the arched span of Narrowsburg Bridge, constructed in 1954 to replace an old covered bridge. The town of Narrowsburg, New York, stands at the New York end of the bridge.

The river widens into Big Eddy, the deepest pool (113 feet) on the Delaware. The current at the surface of Big Eddy flows in a circle, and is in an upstream direction on the left. Big Eddy was a favorite stopping place for timber raftsmen.

289.9. Narrowsburg access area, Pennsylvania. Maintained by the Pennsylvania Fish Commission. Limited parking, paved boat ramp, and trash disposal. Access from U.S. Route 652.

Features

Narrowsburg

This little village on the banks of the Delaware seems not to have changed much in the last century. Originally known as Big Eddy, it was once an important stopping place for timber raftsmen. The New York and Erie Railroad, built through Narrowsburg in 1849, brought permanent settlers and a well-defined business district.

The centerpiece of Narrowsburg was, and still is, the Arlington Hotel, three stories high with broad planked balconies. On his 1892 Delaware canoe adventure J. Wallace Hoff stayed at the Arlington and remarked on the hospitality and attractive waitresses. Today the Arlington Hotel is listed on the National Historic Register, and is occupied by a National Park Service information center and the Delaware Valley Arts Alliance.

Half a mile from the Delaware River bridge at Narrowsburg stands Fort Delaware, a museum of colonial history. The Sullivan County Department of Public Works maintains the fort, which has been constructed according to the specifications of the pioneer settlement at nearby Cushetunk. Fort Delaware, with its log stockades and guardposts, is open to the public in the summer for a nominal fee. Costumed guides demonstrate what life on the eighteenth-century Delaware River frontier might have been like.

Narrowsburg to Barryville

Mile 289.9 to 273.0 (16.9 miles)

This section of the Delaware is dramatically different from those preceding. Below the Big Eddy pool at Narrowsburg, the deepest water in the Delaware between its source and the mouth of Delaware Bay, the river falls over a series of exposed bedrock ledges, creating exciting rapids. Ten-Mile Rift, West Colang Rift, Narrows Falls Rift, and Big Cedar Rift are rated as Class II rapids, while there are 24 rapids of less than Class II. Beginners should consider using a raft, or gaining canoeing experience in calmer water before attempting to run this section.

The river continues through the Appalachian Plateau's geophysical province; outcrops of characteristic shale and sandstone rock occur frequently. The banks are wooded almost entirely by mixed deciduous forests; however, some areas have been cleared for farming or recreational use. This section of the Delaware is the main spawning area for the American shad, an anadromous fish that lives most of its life in the ocean, but migrates into fresh water to spawn. Shad begin their annual run up the Delaware in late spring and arrive here by mid-summer. In the early decades of the twentieth century, the shad migration was almost wiped out by pollution, but in recent years the fish has made a strong comeback.

The Delaware and Hudson (D&H) Canal once paralleled the river on the New York bank below Lackawaxen. Now only its traces remain. The canal was carried across the river on the suspension bridge at Lackawaxen, the hometown of Western writer Zane Grey and the site of the bloody Revolutionary War Battle of Minisink.

There are three public access areas in this section:

Narrowsburg, Pennsylvania, Mile 289.9
Ten-Mile River (Tusten), New York, Mile 284.1
Zane Grey (Lackawaxen), Pennsylvania, Mile 277.6.

13. All boats—even canoes—launched or landed at Pennsylvania Fish Commission access points must bear a valid Pennsylvania registration. Photo by the author.

Many river outfitters maintain private canoe bases along New York Route 97 between Minisink Ford and Barryville.

Virtually all of the lands adjacent to the river are privately owned, and trespassers are not welcome. Camping is allowed only at private campgrounds.

This section is designated as a National Wild and Scenic River, and recreation on the river is under the jurisdiction of the National Park Service. Call 914-252-7100 for the NPS report of river conditions.

River Guide

Map 7

289.9. Narrowsburg access area, Pennsylvania. Maintained by the Pennsylvania Fish Commission. Limited parking, paved boat ramp, privies, and trash disposal. All boats must bear a valid Pennsylvania registration.

289.6. Class I rapids.

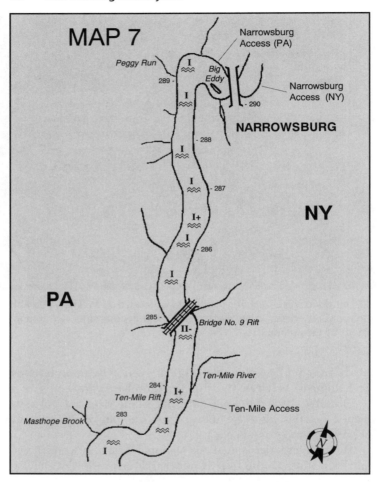

289.5. A small stream enters, Pennsylvania side.

289.3. River becomes shallow and bends sharply left.

289.2. Peggy Run cascades down the cliffs on the Pennsylvania side.

288.7. A small stream enters, Pennsylvania side.

288.3. Eel weir on New York side of river. Class I rapids, with no obstructions, Pennsylvania side.

287.7. Class I rapids; no obstructions.

287.2. A Class I rapids. Rock ledges extend from Pennsylvania side; gravel bars and shallows on left. Main channel with standing waves to 1½ feet is in left center.

286.8. Numerous boulders protrude from water.

286.6. Class I+ rapids in a river narrows. Boulders on right may be hazardous. Main channel is left center. Diminishes to a Class I rapid in .2 mile.

285.6. A Class I rapids with a few submerged and protruding boulders.

285.3. Watch for a "window" in the rocks on the Pennsylvania side.

285.0. Pass under three-truss span of Erie Railroad Bridge (Bridge No. 9).

Enter Bridge No. 9 Rift, a Class II– rapids. Current quickens as it passes under the bridge. Beware of bridge piers. Submerged boulders could easily upset a canoe.

Ten-Mile River Boy Scout Camp, a 14,000-acre reservation operated by the New York City BSA, is on the New York riverbank.

284.0. Ten-Mile River enters, New York side, at a gravel bar extending into the river.

Ten-Mile Rift, a Class I+ rapids—big waves; avoid shallows on the left.

283.9. Ten-Mile River (Tusten) access area, New York, maintained by the National Park Service. There is a muddy landing area, limited parking, picnic tables, trash disposal, and privies. The NPS has an information kiosk here. Access from New York Route 97 at Tusten.

283.6. A boulder ledge across the river presents a Class I rapids. There is a clear channel in left center with standing waves to 1½ feet. Submerged rocks may be a hazard.

283.4. River begins an S turn, first to the right, then to the left.

Map 8

282.7. A Class I rapids at an old eel weir extending from the New York side.

282.4. Masthope Creek enters, Pennsylvania side. River bends sharply left.

The little village of Mast Hope is on the Pennsylvania riverbank. According to tradition this location was the "last hope" for discovering a tree tall enough to become the main mast of the USS *Constitution*, "Old Ironsides." Although much of the

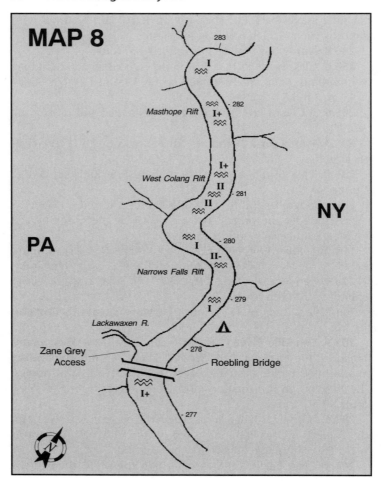

timber cut here in the eighteenth and nineteenth centuries was used in shipbuilding at Philadelphia, it is unlikely that the 104-foot mast of the *Constitution* originated here. The historic Mast Hope plank house is about 100 yards up the road from the river (no access from the river).

282.0. Masthope rift, a Class I+ rapids, beginning with moderate riffles over boulder ledges, then becoming more severe as the river bends slightly right, continuing .4 mile. Considerable maneuvering is required to avoid submerged boulders. The channel on the left is clear but shallow. This is one of the longer rapids encountered on the Delaware.

281.5. Grassy Swamp Brook enters, New York side.

281.4. Enter West Colang Rift, beginning as a Class I+ rapids in a shallows peppered with numerous submerged boulders. The rapids become increasingly severe, continuing .3 mile.

The red-roofed bungalows of Camp Colang, a private camp, are on the Pennsylvania side.

281.1. After a short pause, West Colang Rift becomes a Class II rapids in its final drop, with standing waves greater than 2 feet. Watch out for boulders on the left. Maneuvering is necessary to avoid rocks.

280.5. West Colang Creek enters, Pennsylvania side.

The tailings from an old bluestone quarry are seen in the forest, New York side.

280.3. River bends sharply left around a rocky point.

280.2. A rocky ledge extends from the New York side; there is clear passage to the right.

280.1. A Class I rapids, continuing .3 mile. River is very shallow at low water level.

279.7. After a short pause, the rapids build to Class I+.

279.5. Enter Narrow Falls Rift (Kunkelli Rapids), a Class II– rapids. At moderate and low water level, considerable maneuvering is required to avoid submerged and protruding rocks. The left side is too shallow for passage. The main channel flows in right center, with standing waves to 2 feet, but boulders repeatedly redirect the flow. Capsizing is very common in this rift.

279.1. Narrow Falls Brook enters, New York side.

279.0. New York Route 97 approaches closely on the left, the first major road to do so since Narrowsburg.

278.7. A Class I rapids without significant hazards.

278.5. Camping. Ascalona Campground. Riverside tent sites, privies, picnic tables. (Route 97, Minisink Ford, New York 12719, 914-557-6554.)

278.3. York Lake Creek falls from the New York side.

277.7. The Lackawaxen River enters, Pennsylvania side. At high water level, the Lackawaxen River presents Class II, III, and IV rapids in its course from Honesdale, Pennsylvania.

277.6. Zane Grey access area, Lackawaxen, Pennsylvania, maintained by the Pennsylvania Fish Commission. There is a paved boat ramp, ample parking, picnic tables, telephone, trash disposal,

14. The Erie Railroad bridge across the Lackawaxen River at its confluence with the Delaware, from a 1904 postcard. The trees are bigger today, but the scene is otherwise the same. Note the canoe at the river's edge in the foreground. Courtesy of Greg Pulis.

and privies. The National Park Service maintains an information kiosk here. All boats must bear a valid Pennsylvania registration.

The Zane Grey Inn and Museum, home of author Zane Grey, stands at the access area. (See the features section of this chapter.)

Map 9

277.4. Pass under the Roebling Bridge, built in 1848 to carry the D&H Canal. This bridge is a National Historic Landmark. (See the features section of this chapter.) A riffle on the right side of the river just upstream from the bridge marks the location of a dam, a bane of timber raftsmen and early canoeists, constructed to impound water for the canal. Wooden cribs for the old dam can be seen on the river bottom.

There is a wide gravel bar on the left just past the bridge.

A Class I+ rapids, with tortuous channels and standing waves, begins under the Roebling Bridge.

Enter Otter Eddy; slow water for .6 mile.

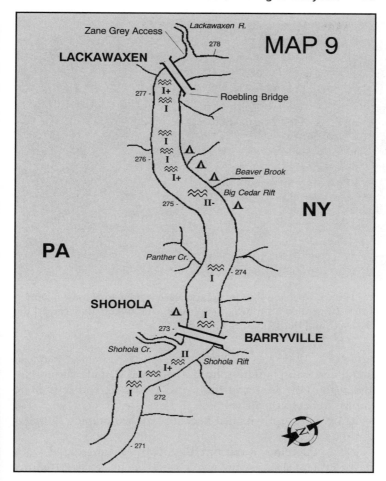

277.1. Stone walls of the D&H Canal rise from the New York riverbank. Remnants of the canal can be seen occasionally from this point to Port Jervis.

276.7. A Class I rapids—beware submerged rocks.

276.3. A Class I rapids with a few submerged and protruding boulders on the right.

276.1. Bald Eagle Observation Site, New York riverbank, turn-out from New York Route 97. Once virtually gone from the Upper Delaware Valley, in recent years bald eagles have made a dramatic

15. Historic Roebling Bridge at Lackawaxen, prior to reconstruction in 1989. Suspended from heavy wire cables, the bridge once carried the Delaware and Hudson Canal. Photo by the author.

comeback. Thanks to wildlife protection laws, habitat management, and transplantation from Alaska and Canada, more than 100 eagles now winter in the Upper Delaware, and several are known to have established nests.

275.9. Enter aptly named Rock Rift, a Class I rapids. Boulders protrude on right.

275.8. Camping. Kittatinny Pine Grove Campground, with riverfront tent sites, privies, picnic tables (an annex to Kittatinny Campground .5 mile downriver). Campers must have rented from Kittatinny Canoes or have a private craft. P.O. Box 95, Route 97, Barryville, New York 12719, 914-557-8611 / 800-356-2852.

275.7. Camping. Landers River Trips has a riverside campground (lean-tos and tent sites) at its Minisink Ford canoe base. Campers must use Landers or private canoes. (1336 Route 97, Narrowsburg, New York 12764, 914-252-3925.)

275.6. Rock Rift ends at a Class I+ rapids. A rock ledge extends diagonally upstream from the New York side. The main channel, with standing waves to 1½ feet, is in the right center.

275.5. Camping. Indian Head Canoes has a campground (tent sites and lean-tos) at its canoe base on the river (Route 97, Barryville, New York 12719, 914-557-8777 / 800-874-2628.)

275.3 Camping. Kittatinny Campgrounds ("Luke's Landing"), operated by Kittatinny Canoes. River and stream front campsites, game areas, laundry, camp store, all facilities. Campers must have rented from Kittatinny or have a private canoe. (P.O. Box 95, Route 97, Barryville, New York 12719, 914-557-8611 / 800-356-2852.)

275.1. Beaver Brook enters, New York side.

Enter Big Cedar Rift, a Class II rapids. The river falls over two ledges, then opens into an area of scattered boulders.

Lunch: Cedar Rapids Inn, New York side.

Camping. Cedar Rapids Kayak and Canoe Outfitters. Riverfront tent sites for canoeists. Hot showers. (P.O. Box 219, Barryville, New York 12719, 914-557-8218.)

275.0. The final ledge of Big Cedar Rift, with a clear channel in the middle. At low water the ledge cannot be penetrated on the right. Haystack waves to 2 feet.

Enter Seely Eddy, extending one mile.

274.5. Camping. Wild and Scenic River Tours has riverfront tent sites at its Barryville canoe base. (166 Route 97, Barryville, New York 12719, 914-557-8723 / 800-836-0366.)

274.0. Little Halfway Brook enters, New York side.

273.9. Panther Brook enters, Pennsylvania side.

273.8. Enter Owens Rift, a Class I rapids continuing .3 mile. The final drop is Class I+, with big waves on the left side of the river.

273.3. A Class I rapids without obstructions. The abutments of the old Shohola Bridge, built originally in 1855 and closed in 1941, are visible on both sides.

273.0. Pass under the three-truss span of the Shohola-Barryville Bridge, constructed in 1941. The villages of Barryville, New York, and Shohola, Pennsylvania, stand at opposite ends of the bridge. There is no public access to or from the river.

Features

Roebling Bridge, Lackawaxen

The old bridge at Lackawaxen is one of six suspension bridges spanning the canoeable portion of the Delaware River. (A suspension bridge is constructed by hanging the roadway from cables suspended across the river.) Downstream from Trenton, the Ben Franklin and Walt Whitman Bridges at Philadelphia and the double-spanned Delaware Memorial Bridge are built on the same principle. Across the country most of the great bridges—the Brooklyn, George Washington, Verrazano Narrows, and Golden Gate—are suspension bridges. But the little bridge at Lackawaxen is special. It is the oldest suspension bridge in America, built by John Roebling, a pioneer of modern civil engineering most famous for his design of the Brooklyn Bridge.

The great stone piers and heavy steel cables of the Lackawaxen bridge seem unnecessarily massive for the narrow roadway. The apparent strength of its construction, however, is a clue to this bridge's history. The D&H Canal, between Honesdale, Pennsylvania, and Rondout, New York, was completed in 1829. The canal route crossed the Delaware River at Lackawaxen, and there the barges were ferried across the current on cables. However, this crossing often bottlenecked commerce on the canal. The crossing could not be made when the river ran high. Ice jams and floods periodically wrecked the towpath on the New York side. The log-rafting industry was at its height, and the huge rafts often crashed into the ferrying canalboats, sparking fistfights and lawsuits. By 1845 the operators of the D&H Canal realized that an alternative had to be found.

The canal firm consulted John A. Roebling, a German-born engineer who was making a name for himself building bridges in Pittsburgh. Roebling's innovative solution to the Lackawaxen crossing was to build the canal above the water.

The bridge was completed in 1849. Steel suspension cables, eight inches in diameter, were spun by hand at the site and strung between Lackawaxen, Pennsylvania, and Minisink Ford, New York. Conventional construction would have required five stone piers, but Roebling's suspension design needed only three. There was plenty of room for timber rafts and ice flows to pass beneath.

Suspended from the cables, atop the stone piers, was the canal itself, a channel 548 feet long, 6 feet deep, and 20 feet across. The bridge was capable of supporting 3,780 tons. Canal barges loaded with coal, weighing 130 tons, routinely crossed the bridge until 1898.

Competition from railroads eventually made the canal operation unprofitable. In 1898 the D&H Canal Company sold the Lackawaxen bridge. The water was drained and the wooden ca-

16. An 1890 view of the Erie Railroad and Roebling Bridge at Lackawaxen. The dam just upstream from the bridge was a serious hazard to timber raftsmen and recreational canoeists of the day. Photo courtesy of the Pike County Historical Society.

nal trough dismantled. The bridge was used as a road crossing, first for horse and buggy, later for automobiles, until 1979. A succession of private owners collected tolls at the crossing. Finally bankrupt, in 1979, the last of these owners abandoned the bridge. The National Park Service acquired the old bridge as part of the Upper Delaware National Scenic and Recreational River and closed it to traffic.

The bridge at Lackawaxen is now a National Historic Landmark. In 1987 the National Park Service began a thorough restoration of the Roebling Bridge. A wooden canal trough was constructed to make the bridge look as it did when barges, not cars, crossed. This unfortunately shrouded the cables and pillars of the bridge from view, but is historically accurate. The wood plank decking was replaced by concrete to allow cars to cross (obviously, not historically accurate), and the stone piers were shielded with heavy wooden armor. The bridge was reopened to vehicle traffic in 1995. There are small parking areas at both ends of the bridge, pedestrian walkways across, and a small museum and information center at the New York end.

When walking or driving across the bridge, one notices that the decking sways and bounces. Yet the strength of the bridge is undiminished; pedestrians and automobiles hardly have begun to tax the piers, cables, and fittings installed by John Roebling 130 years ago. Engineering students are frequently seen inspecting the bridge, as if on a pilgrimage to this milestone of their trade.

As part of its canal operations, the D&H Company built a dam across the Delaware just upstream from the Lackawaxen bridge. This dam, 16 feet high, was "constructed in the most approved scientific manner, to secure strength," according to J. Wallace Hoff. The river passed through a chute in the center of the dam, dropping about 8 feet and setting up huge haystack waves. This was always a trouble spot for timber raftsmen and was among the greatest hazards on the Delaware for early recreational canoeists. The dam is long gone, but some of its base timbers can be seen at low water on the Pennsylvania side of the river, upstream from the bridge.

Zane Grey

The banks of the Delaware do not seem a likely place to inspire legends of the Old West. But it was here at Lackawaxen that Zane Grey wrote most of his 111 books about cowboys and Indians, cavalry and bandits.

Zane Grey, who was born in Ohio in 1872, studied dentistry and opened an office in New York City. He longed for the great outdoors, however, and in 1905, with his brother, he built a big white house on the shores of the Delaware at Lackawaxen. Inspired by a visit to the ranch of frontiersman Colonel C. J. "Buffalo" Jones, Grey was struck with the idea of writing popular fiction about the West. Over the next 14 years, at his home in Lackawaxen, Grey turned out, one after another, his tales of the West, including *Riders of the Purple Sage*, *Desert Gold*, and *The Lone Star Ranger*. More than 100 million copies of his books have been sold, and he has been acclaimed as the most popular author in

17. Tales of the American West were penned by author Zane Grey at his home on the Delaware at Lackawaxen, Pennsylvania. Photo by the author.

the world. In 1918 Zane Grey moved to California where he assisted in the production of many silent and talking movies based on his books. He died in 1939.

Zane Grey's home at Lackawaxen is now maintained as a museum. The treasures and memorabilia collected by Grey, along with his old dentist's drill, are on display. Photographs and paintings of western scenery and people, Navaho rugs, western clothes, Grey's manuscripts, letters, and articles are all assembled for perusal by visitors.

The Zane Grey house and museum is located at the Lackawaxen access area, about 500 yards upstream from the old bridge.

The Battle of Minisink

The Lackawaxen area was wilderness at the time of the American Revolution. The first white settlers came to the area only in 1770. On July 20, 1779, Mohawk War Chieftain Joseph Brandt, fighting on the side of the British, led a party of 27 Tories and 60 Indians on a raid of Minisink (now the Port Jervis area). At

18. The bones of soldiers killed in the Revolutionary War Battle of Minisink lay unburied for 43 years after the battle. This grave is 100 yards south of the Zane Grey access at Lackawaxen, Pennsylvania. Photo by the author.

least four settlers were killed, and houses and barns were burned down. Lieutenant Colonel Benjamin Tusten, on the American side, made quick plans to follow Brandt's raiders and ambush them. About 120 militiamen were mustered to chase Brandt as he retreated up the Delaware.

On the morning of July 22, Brandt's party began to ford the Delaware River at Lackawaxen. The colonial militiamen waited in hiding, but a rifle discharged accidentally, and the ambush was broken. The battle was on. Most of the Continentals took to the high ground on the New York side of the river. The fighting was fierce and lasted throughout the day, ending only when the colonial soldiers, one at a time, made their way into the forest. Forty-seven American militiamen were killed, while only eight of Brandt's raiders were lost.

Not until 1822, when the publication of Tusten's biography aroused public interest in the skirmish, were the bones of the dead collected and taken to Goshen, New York, for burial. In 1847 the skeleton of a Revolutionary soldier was found near the point where the Lackawaxen River joins the Delaware. These remains are now buried in the Unknown Soldier's grave at St. Mark's Lutheran Church at Lackawaxen, a short walk up the road from the Lackawaxen bridge.

Minisink Battleground County Park is located on County Road 168 about one mile up the hill from Route 97 and the old Lackawaxen bridge. This park, site of most of the fighting in the battle, tells the story of the Battle of Minisink by interpretive displays, self-guided trails, and monuments marking the locations of important events. There are picnic sites with grills, rest rooms, and an interpretive center. There is no camping in the park.

Barryville to Port Jervis

Mile 273.0 to 255.3 (17.7 miles)

This section of the Delaware is among the most scenic and challenging. Many river outfitters operate here, and on summer weekends river traffic can be heavy. Do not expect solitude.

The white water of the preceding section continues, though with somewhat less frequency. Shohola Rift, one of the most challenging rapids on the river, and Mongaup Rift, with exceptionally high haystacks, are rated as Class II; about 15 rapids rated at less than Class II also test canoeists' abilities. Beginners should consider rafting this section.

New York Route 97 parallels the river on the left bank the entire distance between Barryville and Port Jervis. There are no significant towns except for Port Jervis and Matamoras at the end of this section. The Erie Railroad runs very close to the river on the Pennsylvania riverbank, while the Delaware and Hudson (D&H) Canal once paralleled the river on the New York side.

The river continues through the Appalachian Plateaus geophysical province. Shale and sandstone bedrock is exposed prominently in several places, most notably at Hawks Nest, where cliffs rise several hundred feet above the river's edge. The riverbanks are mostly heavily forested until the urbanized areas of Port Jervis and Matamoras are approached.

There are three public access areas in this section:

Sparrowbush, New York, Mile 258.3
Matamoras, Pennsylvania, Mile 256.1
Port Jervis Municipal Beach, New York, Mile 255.3.

Virtually all of the lands adjacent to the river are privately owned, and trespassing is not permitted. Except for one primitive camping area on Pennsylvania State Forest lands, camping is allowed only at private campgrounds.

The river in this section (to Sparrowbush) is part of the Upper

19. Canoeists enter Shohola Rift, a Class II rapids just downstream from the Shohola-Barryville Bridge. Photo by the author.

Delaware National Scenic and Recreational River, under the jurisdiction of the National Park Service. Call 914-252-7100 for the NPS report of river conditions.

River Guide

Map 10

273.0. Pass under the Shohola-Barryville Bridge, constructed in 1941 to replace an older bridge 1/4 mile upstream. The present bridge is at the site of an old ferry crossing.

The villages of Barryville, New York, and Shohola, Pennsylvania, stand at opposite ends of the bridge. There is no public access to or from the river.

Lunch: Reber's Sea Gull Restaurant and Motel; Barryville Coffee Shop and Ice Cream (New York end of bridge).

Halfway Brook enters, New York side, just downstream from the bridge. Gravel bars and shallows on the left.

272.9. Enter Shohola Rift (also known as Mitchie Falls), a Class II rapids extending .5 mile. This is one of the longest and

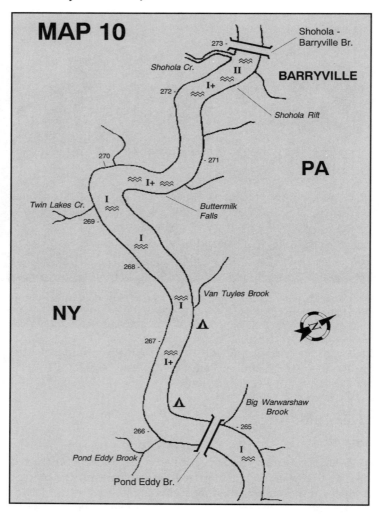

MAP 10

Shohola - Barryville Br.

273 -

Shohola Cr.

II

BARRYVILLE

I+

272 -

Shohola Rift

270

- 271

PA

I+

Twin Lakes Cr.

I

Buttermilk Falls

269 -

I

268 -

Van Tuyles Brook

NY

I

267 -

I+

Big Warwarshaw Brook

266 -

- 265

I

Pond Eddy Brook

Pond Eddy Br.

most challenging rapids to be found on the Delaware River. The clearest channel is on the left.

272.8. Shohola Creek enters, Pennsylvania side, from a steep ravine. Shohola Falls, dropping nearly 100 feet over several ledges, is located on Shohola Creek about 1.5 miles from the Delaware River. The rapids in the Delaware River here are often mistakenly referred to as Shohola Falls.

Rapids become more severe with numerous boulders obstructing the channel. The river is deepest in the center here, but canoeists must navigate between boulders.

272.7. The rapids abate for a short distance, then continue. At low water the left side is too shallow to navigate. Cliffs on the left are known as Little Hawks Nest.

272.2. Shohola Rift continues. The main channel, with standing waves to 2 feet, is in the right center. The left side is very shallow at low water. There is a wide rock ledge along the left bank just downstream from the end of Shohola Rift. This is a good place to pull over and bail canoes of the water gained while passing through the rift.

271.9. The final falls of Shohola Rift, at this point a Class I rapids, over boulders and ledges.

271.8. Enter Handsome Eddy. Slow water for one mile.

270.6. Center and left of the river are very shallow. At low water numerous boulders protrude in a line down the middle.

270.5. Begin Buttermilk Falls, a Class I+ rapids. Watch for numerous protruding and submerged boulders.

270.2. Buttermilk Falls continues over a series of three ledges. The last drop is the most severe. The main current runs from left center to center, but leads directly toward a big submerged boulder in the very middle of the river. Big waves!

270.0. Enter Quicks Eddy (Eckharts Eddy), continuing .5 mile. Camp Tel-Yehudah, a private camp, is located on the New York riverbank.

269.9. Quicks Eddy river rest area, with picnic tables and privies, New York side, maintained by the National Park Service. This is not a boat launch area. NPS ranger offices (South District), locally known as the "Coop," are up a short trail from the landing (access also from New York Route 97).

269.7. River makes a right angle turn to the left.

269.5. Carrs Rock Brook (Twin Lakes Creek) enters, Pennsylvania side.

269.4. A Class I rapids, dubbed Lost Channel Rift by J. Wallace Hoff on his trip down the Delaware in 1892, continues .4 mile. A few protruding boulders may be a hazard.

The community of Parkers Glen, a center of the local bluestone industry in the 1800s, once stood above the railroad on the Pennsylvania riverbank. Today only a cemetery and a few foundations remain (no access from the river).

268.5. A Class I rapids, no obstructions.

268.2. Parking area along New York Route 97 atop the bluffs on the New York side, with picnic tables and trash barrels.

267.8. Van Tuyles Brook enters, New York side.

267.6. An old eel weir in the center of the river, very shallow over the wings. Gravel bars and shallows on the left.

Pass under power line marked by red balls.

267.5. Landers River Trips and Kittatinny Canoes landings, New York side.

267.4. A Class I rapids without obstructions. Submerged boulders may be a hazard at low water.

267.3. Camping. Jerry's Three River Canoes (P.O. Box 7, Pond Eddy, New York 12770, 914-557-6078) has campsites at its canoe base on New York Route 97.

266.9. A Class I+ rapid in a constriction of the river, continues .8 mile.

266.0. Wide rock ledges extend into the river from the Pennsylvania side.

Camping. Indian Head Canoes operates a campground (tent sites and lean-tos) at its Pond Eddy canoe base. (Route 97, Barryville, New York 12719, 914-557-8777 / 800-874-2628.)

265.8. Pond Eddy Brook enters, Pennsylvania side, via a picturesque stone tunnel beneath the Erie tracks.

265.2. Big Warwarshaw Brook enters, New York side.

Though no "official" access, Pond Eddy, New York, can be reached via a steep trail to New York Route 97 at the mouth of the brook.

265.1. Pass under Pond Eddy Bridge, a double-truss steel bridge built in 1926. A suspension bridge was built 1/2 mile upstream in the early 1870s but was washed away in the Pumpkin Flood of 1903, after which the banks and islands of the Delaware were littered with hundreds of pumpkins left by the floodwaters.

The once thriving community of Pond Eddy is on the Pennsylvania riverbank. This was the center of the local bluestone slate industry, and the village was once called Flagstone. A huge slab of bluestone quarried here was placed in front of City Hall in New York City.

Lunch: Nolan's River Inn and Millbrook Inn, Pond Eddy, New York.

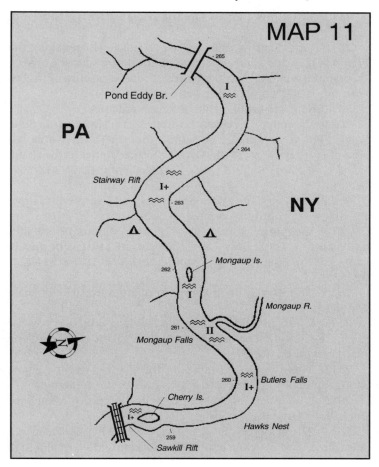

Map 11

264.9. Very shallow on the left; many boulders protrude from the river.

264.5. A Class I rapids, with protruding and submerged boulders across the river. An eel weir on the left may be a hazard at low water.

River bends to the right.

264.3. Pass under a cable crossing marked by orange balls.

Fish Cabin Brook enters, New York side.

263.4. Kittatinny Canoes landing (Knights Eddy), New York side.

263.3. Enter Stairway Rift, a Class I+ rapids. Ledges along the Pennsylvania side are in the configuration of a staircase, giving this rapid its name. The rift extends .2 mile as a series of ledges, with the main channel on the left.

263.0. Stairway Brook enters, Pennsylvania side.

262.9. Camping. Buckhorn Natural Area (Pennsylvania State Forest). Primitive camping by permit from the Pennsylvania Bureau of Forestry (717-424-3001), or NPS ranger office at the Coop. (New York Route 97, 3.5 miles north of Pond Eddy, 914-557-02220.)

262.7. Enter Knights Eddy, also called Dickersons Eddy; slow-moving water continues .8 mile.

262.5. Camping. Landers River Trips campground (tent sites and lean-tos), all services. Campers must use Landers or private canoes. (1336 Route 97, Narrowsburg, New York 12764, 914-252-3925.)

262.1. The river is bounded on both sides by slabs of shale bedrock.

262.0. Upstream end of Mongaup Island, a brushy gravel bar extending .2 mile. The channel on either side is clear, with the main current on the left.

261.9. There are Class I rapids in the channel to the right of Mongaup Island, ending with a drop over an old eel weir.

261.3. A buoy advises "WARNING!—Rapids ahead—Wear your life jacket!" Heed this advice!

261.0. The Mongaup River enters, New York side. There is a huge stone and concrete abutment supporting the Erie Railroad on the Pennsylvania side.

Enter Mongaup Rift, also known as Mitchels Falls, a Class II rapid. Ledges and shallows extend from the New York side, with the current pressed against the Pennsylvania side. The rapids begin over boulder ledges, then funnel into a chute where the biggest standing waves to be found on the Delaware are formed. The channel through the chute is clear, but canoes will almost surely take on water in the three-foot haystacks. BIG WAVES!

260.0. River bends sharply to the right. A large gravel point bar, known as Butlers Island, has developed on the right side.

Enter Butlers Falls, a Class I+ rapid. The current flows very near

20. A sign posted by the National Park Service gives good advice to canoeists about to enter Mongaup Rift, a Class II rapids. Photo by Courtenay Kling.

21. Waves up to three feet high give canoeists a wild ride at Mongaup Rift. Photo by Courtenay Kling.

the New York side without obstructions; standing waves 2½ feet high make for a wild ride. Rock ledges extend from the left.

Hawks Nest Mountain rises steeply from the river on the New York side. A drive along New York Route 97 over Hawks Nest Mountain is spectacular.

This area was known as the "cellar hole" to timber raftsmen because of the 250-foot sheer cliffs on the left. The cellar hole was a trap for rafts in high water, and raftsmen struggled to keep their crafts as close as possible to the Pennsylvania side to avoid being dashed on the rocks.

259.9. Enter Long Track Eddy. The Erie tracks run atop the Pennsylvania riverbank.

The Hawk's Nest Restaurant perches high above Butlers Falls on New York Route 97, not accessible from the river. There are spectacular views from the informal dining room.

In the 1800s the D&H Canal ran against the cliffs 40 feet above the river. Walls of the canal can be seen along the river's edge, New York side. (See the features section of this chapter.)

259.7. Hay Rock, so called because a ferry hauled hay here for a nearby farm, stands prominently on the cliffs on the New York side.

258.9. Upstream end of Cherry Island (also known as Sawmill Rift Island), which extends .2 mile. The main channel flows right of the island in a Class I+ rapid, with the best passage in the center of the channel. The left channel is shallow but passable at moderate water level. There is a Class I rapid with standing waves to 1½ feet at the downstream end of the left channel.

Sparrowbush Creek enters the left channel (New York side).

258.7. Downstream end of Cherry Island.

Enter Sawmill Rift, also known as Sawyers Falls or Millrift Rapids, a Class I+ rapids. At low water there are numerous submerged and protruding boulders, with shallows extending from the downstream end of the island. The best passage, with standing waves to 2 feet, is in the center of the channel.

The little community of Millrift, Pennsylvania, is very close to the water on the right. A ferry operated here in the last century.

Sawyerskill Creek (known also as Bushkill Creek) enters, Pennsylvania side.

Sawmill Rift was celebrated in verse by Robert "Boney" Quillan, a raftsman-poet of the nineteenth century:

22. Anglers test their skill at the aptly named Elephant Feet Rocks, near Sparrowbush, New York. Photo by the author.

We sailed around Old Butler's,
And little did we fear;
Until we came to Sawmill Rift—
And slammed against the pier.

258.4. Pass under a bridge carrying the Erie Railroad. First built as a wooden structure in 1850, the bridge was replaced later by the present steel span. Sawmill Rift ends in a Class I rapid.

The railroad bridge marks the downstream boundary of the Upper Delaware National Scenic and Recreational River.

Map 12

258.3. Sparrowbush access area, Sparrowbush, New York. Maintained by the New York Department of Environmental Conservation. Natural beach for boat launch, limited parking, no facilities. Access from Hook Road off New York Route 97.

Remnants of the D&H Canal are found beside the dirt road that leads along the access area.

A cliff aptly known as Elephant Feet Rocks rises from the water on the Pennsylvania side.

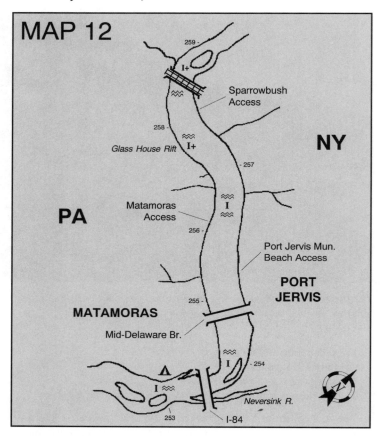

258.0. Golf course on New York riverbank—watch for errant balls in the river.

257.9. An eel weir extends across the river. Canoeists should stay as close to the Pennsylvania side as possible.

Enter Glass House Rift, a Class I+ rapids. In the early 1800s a glass factory operated atop the cliffs. The rapids end with big standing waves beneath the towering Glass House Cliffs.

A broad gravel bar extends from the New York side.

257.2. Shingle Kill enters, New York side.

Enter Jerrys Eddy, a slow stretch of water extending one mile.

256.5. Silver Canoes landing (Sparrowbush), New York side.

Whitewater Willies landing, New York side.

Indian Head Canoes landing (Matamoras), Pennsylvania side.

Jerrys Three Rivers Canoes landing, Pennsylvania side.
Kittatinny Canoes landing, Pennsylvania side.
Landers River Trips landing, Pennsylvania side.
256.4. A series of rock ledges extend from the New York side almost across the river. There is a Class I rapids with standing waves to 1¹/₂ feet along the Pennsylvania side.
256.1. Matamoras access area, Matamoras, Pennsylvania. Maintained by the Pennsylvania Fish Commission. There is a wide paved ramp, ample parking, sanitary facilities, trash disposal, and fresh water. All boats must bear a valid Pennsylvania registration.
255.5. The High Point monument stands atop the Kittatinny Ridge, straight ahead. At 1803 feet, High Point is the highest point in the state of New Jersey.
255.3. Municipal Beach Access, Port Jervis, New York, maintained by the City of Port Jervis. There is a dirt boat ramp, swimming area, privies. Access from Ferry Street, Port Jervis. Private canoe launching is permitted, but commercial access is not.
This is the site of the old Mapes Ferry, which crossed here in the nineteenth century.

Features

Delaware and Hudson Canal

Unlike Pennsylvania's Delaware Canal and New Jersey's Delaware and Raritan Canal, which parallel the Delaware River below Easton and are preserved in state parks, the Delaware and Hudson (D&H) Canal remains only in traces along its course between Honesdale, Pennsylvania, and Rondout, New York. Finding and retracing segments of the old D&H Canal can be an exciting adventure.

Construction on the D&H Canal began in 1827 to enable shipment of Pennsylvania mountain coal to the tidewater Hudson River and New York City. The first barge passed through in 1829, followed by an almost endless stream of commerce until 1898 when the D&H Canal finally succumbed to competition from the railroads. There were three sections to the D&H Canal: the Lackawaxen section, which paralleled the Lackawaxen River from Honesdale to Lackawaxen; the Delaware section, between Minisink Ford and Port Jervis; and the Neversink section, between Port Jervis and Rondout on the Hudson.

23. Remnants such as this wall is all that remains of the Delaware and Hudson Canal, which once paralleled the river from Lackawaxen to Port Jervis. Photo by the author.

The Delaware section began where the canal crossed the river between Lackawaxen, Pennsylvania, and Minisink Ford, New York. Initially, the D&H Canal Company constructed a dam to impound the Delaware River so that barges could be towed across the river upstream of the dam. This method, however, was rife with failure, frustration, and lawsuits. Extreme variations in water level, ice flows, and collisions with timber rafts forced an innovative solution upon the canal company. In 1848 the Delaware suspension aqueduct, designed by John A. Roebling, was constructed to carry canal barges over the river at Lackawaxen. This remarkable bridge stands today as the most prominent remaining feature of the D&H Canal.

Most of the way between Minisink Ford and Port Jervis the D&H Canal paralleled the Delaware River and was separated from it only by a stone berm. Today New York Route 97 between Minisink Ford and Barryville is built directly upon the canal right-of-way. In numerous places the carefully laid stone walls that originally carried the canal can be seen underlying the modern highway. The canal route and New York Route 97 likewise coincide in several segments between Barryville and Port Jervis. Near the entrance to the modern Barryville-Shohola Bridge, a historical marker identifies the location of a D&H Canal dry dock. The remains of two lift locks can be discovered also in this vicinity.

Between Barryville and Port Jervis old stonework of the D&H Canal can be seen occasionally along the river. At the Mongaup River, the canal passed through the largest of four aqueducts between Lackawaxen and Port Jervis. Mongaup Village, today just a name on a map, was an important center of canal activity with a dry dock, company buildings, and several canal control facilities. One of the best-preserved lift locks stands just a few feet from the river a short way downstream from the Mongaup River.

The course of the D&H Canal through the treacherous Hawks Nest was a considerable engineering feat. Though only traces remain, the canal clung to the New York cliffs atop a 40-foot-high hand-laid stone wall. Butlers Lock, just at the sharpest bend in the river, controlled access to this section of the canal. The foundation of the locktender's house and traces of the stone walls of the canal berm are all that remain today.

Between Cherry Island and the Sawmill Rift railroad bridge the D&H Canal maintained another operations center. This location, known as Bolten Basin, was the scene of the worst of many calamities to befall the D&H Canal. In October 1882 two heavily loaded Erie Railroad flatcars crashed through the iron bridge spanning the canal. Several more cars in the train followed, dragging with them their cargoes, telegraph poles, and the remains of the bridge. The train landed squarely in the canal, forcing its closure for an extended period.

Precariously perched next to the Delaware River, the D&H Canal between Lackawaxen and Port Jervis was especially vulnerable to minor disasters. Frequently the retaining wall would break, draining the canal into the river and stranding commerce. In the event of such emergencies, special repair scows were on 24-hour standby duty. These boats had right-of-way over all other barges and carried workmen with equipment and materials to repair any damage. In several places guard locks could be closed in order to localize drainage from the canal.

Even with these precautions, serious mishaps occurred. On August 5, 1885, a strong northeast storm dumped heavy rain on the Port Jervis area, flooding the D&H Canal. The numerous waste weirs, designed to vent excess water, were filled with brush and driftwood. At the mouth of Shinglekill Brook, at Bolten Basin, the canal wall breached. Several canalboats became caught in the surge and wedged together near the break, temporarily stemming the tide. But water continued to flood the canal, and a second breach opened a thousand feet upstream from the first. Two hundred feet of canal bank was washed away. Six canalboats were destroyed, and fourteen others were damaged.

The D&H Canal ultimately became unprofitable: on the other side of the river, the New York and Erie Railroad commanded more and faster traffic, and revenue from the shipment of coal on the canal declined steadily in the last half of the nineteenth century. To make up the loss the canal company encouraged excursions on the canal. Tourists and sightseers could take specially outfitted barges up the canal into the scenic Delaware Valley. Excursion boats did indeed become popular, but they only postponed the inevitable. In 1898 the D&H Canal was abandoned.

Early recreational canoeists paddled along, in the words of J. Wallace Hoff, with "the ever attendant noise of horns and shoutings, together with the choice vocabulary of captains and mule drivers"; today canoeists encounter only traces and memories of the D&H Canal.

The New York and Erie Railroad

The rails run close to the river all the way from Hancock to Tusten, where they cross to Pennsylvania at Bridge No. 9. From there the tracks closely parallel the Delaware to Sawmill Rift, where the river is spanned by a heavy steel bridge, then continue into Port Jervis and points south. Occasionally a long freight rumbles by, breaking the river's solitude or shaking campers like an earthquake. For the first 75 miles of the Delaware River, canoeists are never far from the New York and Erie Railroad.

In 1825 the Erie Canal opened the American Midwest via its route between the Hudson River at Albany and Lake Erie. It wasn't long before entrepreneurs realized that steam locomotives would someday be faster, more efficient, and more profitable. Plans were unveiled in 1835 for the construction of a railroad from New York City to the shores of Lake Erie, a distance of more than 400 miles, and an enormous undertaking, both physically and financially.

The president of the New York and Erie Railroad had promised that trains would be running to Port Jervis before 1848, and he was a man to keep his word. But it wasn't until the last day

of 1847 that the first locomotive arrived in Port Jervis. The locomotive—called the "Eleazar Lord"—and two flatcars carrying dozens of dignitaries were moved into position east of the Neversink
River for a triumphant entry into the village. But the tracks had
not yet been laid over the Neversink trestle. Well after dark the
trainmen, together with local citizens, worked rapidly to get the
track in place. A few minutes before 11:00 P.M. all but one piece
had been laid, and that rail had to be cut to fit. At only 17 minutes to midnight on December 31, 1847, the rails to Port Jervis
were finally completed. The little train chugged into town to begin a grand party.

From Port Jervis the New York and Erie Railroad was to wind
north along the Delaware River. Compared to the south bank,
the north bank of the Delaware River is quite gentle; however, this
side was already occupied by the D&H Canal. By action in the
state legislature and courts, the D&H Canal Company preempted
the railroad from occupying the same bank. So the Erie right-of-
way had to be carved out of the rock cliffs on the Pennsylvania
side of the river, the railroad crossing the river just above Glass
House Rocks near Sawmill Rift. In some places workmen were suspended in baskets from the cliffs. They drilled blast holes in the
rock and were hauled to safety after the fuse was lighted.

There was a good deal of animosity between the railroad construction crews and the canal bargemen on the opposite bank.
There were countless brawls, and it was not unheard-of for shots
to be fired across the river. Railroad crews learned to time their
powder blasts with the passage of canal barges, so that the barges
and their occupants were showered with rocks and dust. In spite
of all this, railroad construction progressed rapidly, and Bingham-
ton, New York, was reached by the end of 1848. Finally, in 1851,
the railroad was completed to Dunkirk, New York, on Lake Erie:
the East Coast and the American interior were linked.

Since the time of the Roman Empire, wagon axles were made
a standard 4 feet 8¹/₂ inches long, allowing the wheels to follow
the same ruts in the road. The first railroads in England followed
this tradition, as did most of the early lines in the United States.
But the builders of the New York and Erie Railroad favored a 6-
foot gauge to allow heavier traffic and to deter competition from
standard gauge roads. In its first decades specially designed Erie
locomotives ran between New York, up the Delaware Valley, to
Dunkirk on rails 6 feet apart. Inevitably, and at great expense,

the Erie standardized its track to be compatible with the equipment and lines used in the rest of the country.

The early days of railroading on the New York and Erie were hazardous. The telegraph had not yet been invented, so there was no effective way to communicate activity along a line. Lapses in communication often resulted in disaster. The worst crash occurred during the Civil War, when a train carrying 800 Confederate prisoners in 19 wooden freight cars slammed head-on with a locomotive hauling 50 cars of coal. Seventy-five souls perished in the wreck. Their remains were buried in a common grave along the tracks in Shohola. In April 1868 at Parkers Glen, several derailed passenger cars plunged off the cliffs onto the rocks along the river where they burst into flames. Forty passengers were killed and another 75 injured. Terrible wrecks also occurred at Shohola, Millrift, and Bolten Basin.

Many of the towns and hamlets along the Upper Delaware grew around the New York and Erie Railroad. Hancock, Lordville, Long Eddy, Hankins, Callicoon, Narrowsburg, Lackawaxen, Shohola, Millrift, and Port Jervis grew or survived because of their location by the tracks. Each of these towns and hamlets boasted a depot, many of which remain standing.

The New York and Erie tracks, now operated by Conrail, have been upgraded to modern standards. There are frequent freight trains and regular passenger service. Occasionally, a great steam locomotive hauling an excursion train rumbles up the Delaware Valley, echoing the whistles and roar heard there for 136 years.

Port Jervis/Matamoras

It may seem paradoxical that a city so far from the sea could be called a port. Yet Port Jervis is accurately named, for it was once an important canalboat basin and layover for replenishing supplies and resting mules. "P.J.," or "Port," is about halfway along the route of the old D&H Canal. The chief engineer behind the canal was John B. Jervis.

Sparse settlement of the Port Jervis area began in the mid-eighteenth century at Carpenters Point, where the Neversink River meets the Delaware. Among these settlers were John Decker and his family. The historic Decker home, known today as Fort Decker, was rebuilt after an Indian raid in 1779. Now owned and maintained by the Minisink Valley Historical Society, Fort Decker is open to the public on an irregular basis.

After the D&H Canal was opened in 1828, the community of Port Jervis began to thrive. In 1851 the Erie Railroad completed its line between Hoboken, New Jersey, and Dunkirk, New York. Port Jervis, which was about halfway along the route, quickly became a commercial center. Port Jervis was very much a railroad town, so with the closing of the canal and decline of the railroads, the city became less vital. The majestic old railroad terminal, abandoned for many years, has been renovated recently and stands only a few blocks from the Mid-Delaware Bridge. With the construction of Interstate Route 84 and the growth of outdoor recreation in the vicinity, the fortunes of Port Jervis have stabilized. Today Port Jervis is a pleasant small city.

The link across the river between Port Jervis and Pike County, Pennsylvania, has always been an important one. Soon after the first settlers arrived, Benjamin Carpenter and Courtright Middaugh began operating scow ferries from Carpenters Point (where the Neversink River meets the Delaware) to the future site of Matamoras. After the construction of the D&H Canal in 1829, the community of Port Jervis began to grow rapidly at its present location, and the Carpenters Point ferry was abandoned. In 1830 Simeon Westfall began operating a ferry upstream from the river bend, and in 1844 one Gabriel Mapes started a ferry service at River Mile 255.3, which docked at present-day Ferry Street, Port Jervis. The ferry was nothing more than a crude wooden platform 55 feet long and 10^1/$_2$ feet wide. It was guided by an overhead rope and propelled by the force of the current and by poling against the bottom. Oliver S. Dimmick purchased the Mapes Ferry in 1846. Dimmick was proud to advertise that "careful ferrymen are constantly in attendance, and the rates are very low. The large elephant attached to Turner's menagerie was carried over the Delaware River on this ferry in perfect safety."

Like many of the ferry communities along the Delaware River, Port Jervis and Matamoras soon outgrew the slow-moving scows. In 1854 a 40-foot-wide covered bridge, with separate lanes for foot, wagon, and railroad traffic, was completed. Although the railroad was never installed, this bridge served well until 1870, when it was blown off its pilings in a strong gale. A new wire suspension bridge was completed in 1872; three years later an ice gorge lifted this bridge away and carried it downriver. In a mere 68 days a second suspension bridge was erected to replace the first. This bridge lasted until 1903 when it was destroyed in the famous Pumpkin Flood, so called because of the many pumpkins left along the river after the floodwaters receded. A double-truss iron bridge was completed at the site the following year and was used until 1939 when it was replaced by the modern Mid-Delaware Bridge. All the Port Jervis/Matamoras bridges were privately owned until 1922, when public sentiment forced the sale of the bridge to the state so that it could be operated as a tollfree crossing.

Matamoras, Pennsylvania, immediately across the Delaware from Port Jervis, grew along with Port Jervis and has always been a satellite community. Unlike Port Jervis, however, Matamoras is laid out in blocks separated by streets and alleys.

There are many services accessible to canoeists in Port Jervis and Matamoras. Among these is the Flo-Jean Restaurant in Port Jervis, which has become a local landmark. Incorporating the old tollhouse of the Mid-Delaware Bridge, Flo-Jean's is renowned for excellent cuisine. Inside are many historical photographs and newspaper clippings of the Port Jervis–Matamoras area, a collection of early American dolls and carriages, antique art, and the old toll panel listing the crossing charges for various vehicles, animals, and people. There are many other services in both Port Jervis and Matamoras, including restaurants, groceries, sports shops, and hospitals.

Port Jervis to Dingmans Ferry

Mile 255.3 to 238.4 (16.9 miles)

The river changes dramatically as it bends sharply south at Port Jervis. The white water of the previous 40 miles is left behind, and the river becomes wider and generally deeper. Only one rapid, found in the tortuous channels around Quicks Island, presents any real difficulty. This section is excellent for beginners.

The river is deflected south at Port Jervis by the rocks of the Ridge and Valley geophysical province, a band of wrinkled mountains that extends between Vermont and Alabama. The Ridge and Valley Province includes the Kittatinny Mountains in New Jersey and the famous Blue Ridge in Virginia and North Carolina. Facing downstream, the Ridge and Valley Province is on the left, while the Pocono Mountain portion of the Appalachian Plateaus Province is on the right.

The islands in this section differ noticeably from the low gravel bars farther upstream. Here the islands rise 15 or 20 feet above the river level on high silty banks. Mature forests have developed on the islands, which are rarely inundated during floods. Towering tulip poplar trees, with an undergrowth of fern, make the islands well worth a stop. These river islands were deposited when the great continental glacier melted about 15,000 years ago, swelling the flow of the river with gravel and silt. The river basin itself is filled with the stony debris left by the melting glacier, and bedrock is exposed in very few places.

Much of the land adjacent to the river has been cleared for farming. Some of it is still used as such; however, other areas have reverted to forest. This is excellent habitat for deer, which are frequently seen along the river's edge on either side. Black bear have been making a comeback in recent years, and it is not uncommon for canoeists to see them along the riverbanks. Many species of waterfowl make their nests on the riverbanks and islands.

The river valley here was once inhabited by the Lenni Lenape, or Delaware Indians, and their predecessors. The Indians were here when European settlers first came to the valley, and archaeological exploration has revealed much earlier habitation. In the late eighteenth century the Lenape waged unrelenting war against the settlers. Tom Quick of Milford countered with a personal campaign of vengeance which has become a local legend. This area is also known for conservationist Gifford Pinchot, who lived in Milford in the early decades of the present century, and for Dingmans Bridge, one of the last private toll bridges in America.

Excepting the first few miles, the river and adjacent lands in this section are within the Delaware Water Gap National Recreation Area (DWGNRA), which is part of the National Park system. Port Jervis, New York, and Matamoras and Milford, Pennsylvania, are the main towns in this area. U.S. Route 209 roughly parallels the river on the Pennsylvania side. The New Jersey side is sparsely populated, and virtually no services are available.

There are public access sites at:

Port Jervis Municipal Beach, New York, Mile 255.3
Milford, Pennsylvania, Mile 246.2
Dingmans Ferry, Pennsylvania, Mile 238.4.

Camping for one night only via canoe is permitted at designated primitive campsites on river islands and on the riverbanks within DWGNRA. Rangers are known to issue tickets to persons camping at unauthorized locations, or not on a river trip. Sites are marked by an NPS camp sign. Each site has a metal fire grate, and some have privies or pit toilets, but there are no other improvements, so be prepared to rough it. Since there is no road access, camping is only among fellow canoeists. Private full-service campgrounds may be found at Matamoras and near Milford.

River Guide

Map 13

255.3. Municipal Beach Access, Port Jervis, New York, maintained by the City of Port Jervis. There is a dirt boat ramp, swimming area, privies. Access from Ferry Street, Port Jervis. Private canoe launching is permitted, but commercial access is not.

This is the site of the old Mapes Ferry, which crossed here in the nineteenth century.

255.2. Bridge abutments on both riverbanks and the remnant

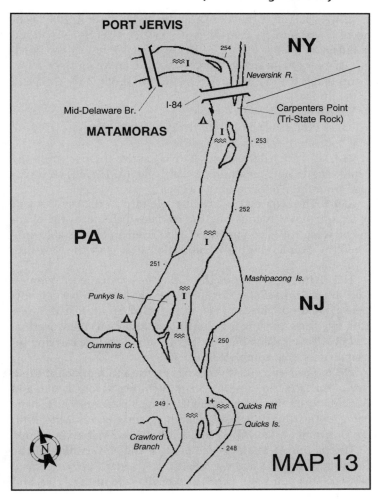

PORT JERVIS

254

NY

Neversink R.

Mid-Delaware Br.   I-84   Carpenters Point
(Tri-State Rock)

MATAMORAS

· 253

· 252

PA   251 ·

Mashipacong Is.

Punkys Is.   **NJ**

Cummins Cr.   · 250

249 ·   I+   Quicks Rift

Quicks Is.

Crawford
Branch   · 248

MAP 13

of a pier in the center of the river mark the temporary location of the Mid-Delaware Bridge during construction of the present bridge in 1939. The old bridge was floated upriver and anchored here while the new bridge was being built.

Power lines pass overhead.

254.8. River widens and becomes quite shallow, with a moderate riffle over the gravel bottom. There is an eel weir near the New York riverbank.

254.7. Pass under the Mid-Delaware Bridge, built in 1939, connecting Matamoras, Pennsylvania, and Port Jervis, New York, population 9,060 (1990). (See the features section of the previous chapter.) Flo-Jean's Restaurant, a local landmark since 1929, incorporates the old toll house on the Port Jervis, New York, end of the bridge.

Shallows or gravel bars on left.

254.6. Numbers painted on the concrete bulkhead, New York side, indicate elevation above sea level.

254.3. A rock ledge extends halfway across the river from the Pennsylvania side, presenting a Class I rapids. There is clear passage around the left end of the ledge.

254.1. The river makes a right-angle turn to the right. A pair of brushy gravel islands hug the outside of the turn; the channel between the island and New York riverbank is passable only when the river level is high. Bare shale ledges plate the New York riverbank.

The right-angle turn of the Delaware was called "Symme's Clip" by old-time timber raftsmen. During high water, when rafts were floated downstream, the river boiled up against the New York riverbank, making for difficult and hazardous maneuvering.

253.7. Pass under a high concrete and steel bridge carrying Interstate Route 84, completed in 1973.

253.6. The Neversink River enters on the left. A principal tributary of the Delaware, the Neversink is renowned for Class III and IV white water that rages through a gorge upstream. The Lenape name for the Neversink was Mahacamac, and the confluence with the Delaware was known to colonial settlers as Mahacamac Fork.

The peninsula at the confluence of the Neversink and the Delaware is called Carpenters Point. Carpenter's Ferry operated between this point and the Pennsylvania side in the 1700s and early 1800s.

A cemetery occupies most of the peninsula, final resting place for members of many of the founding families of the area, including the Deckers, Quicks, and Westfalls. The grave marker of Benjamin Carpenter, dated 1826, can be found at the very end of the cemetery, under the I-84 bridge.

Tri-State Rock, a small stone monument with an embedded bronze benchmark, stands at the water's edge at the very tip of Carpenters Point. Tri-State Rock marks the intersection of the boundaries of New York, New Jersey, and Pennsylvania. The little

24. Tri-State Rock, on Carpenters Point at the confluence of the Neversink River and the Delaware at Port Jervis, marks the intersection of the boundaries of New Jersey, New York, and Pennsylvania. Photo by the author.

monument is actually located in three states. A somewhat larger monument higher on the rocks (under the I-84 bridge) cites the engineers who surveyed the boundary.

253.5. Camping. Tri-State Canoe base, private access and campsite, Pennsylvania riverbank just downstream from I-84 bridge. Access from river and Shay Lane (off I-84). Full facilities.

253.3. Symmes Islands, left side. The channel between the islands and New Jersey riverbank is shallow and barely passable at moderate river level.

253.1. A Class I rapids with moderate standing waves and a few submerged boulders. The rapids end at an eel weir, in use as of 1996.

252.8. Kittatinny Canoes landing, Pennsylvania side.

251.9. Upstream end of Mashipacong Island, extending 2.5 miles downstream. The channel between the island and New Jersey riverbank is usually dry, visible only as a swampy pass through the forest.

251.8. A Class I rapids with moderate standing waves flows right to left, then left to right. Submerged boulders near the end of the rapid may be a hazard.

251.3. A small unnamed creek enters, Pennsylvania side.

250.8. Upstream end of Punkys Island. The main channel is left of Punkys Island, although the right channel (Pennsylvania side) is also passable.

There is a Class I rapids in the channel to the left of the island.

250.4. From the main (left) channel a secondary passage cuts diagonally through Punkys Island.

250.1. Camping. River Beach campground, access from river and U.S. Route 209. Full facilities. Operated by Kittatinny Canoes; campers must have rented from Kittatinny or have a private canoe. (P.O. Box 95, Route 97, Barryville, New York 12719, 914-557-8611 / 800-356-2852.)

Cummins Creek enters, Pennsylvania side.

250.0. Downstream end of Punkys Island. Fast water, no obstructions.

The Delaware Water Gap National Recreation Area (DWGNRA) and Middle Delaware National Scenic and Recreational River begin here. From this point to just south of the Delaware Water Gap, use of the river and adjacent lands is under the jurisdiction of the National Park Service.

249.9. A power line marked by red balls crosses the river.

249.2. Downstream end of Mashipacong Island.

Camping. There is one NPS primitive campsite at the downstream point of Mashipacong Island.

248.8. Enter Quicks Rift, a Class I+ rapids, one of the trickier rapids to be found on the Delaware. There are no obstructions, but the current flows around gravel bars and Quicks Island. The current, which changes directions suddenly and forms eddies and boils, is capable of upsetting canoes or pushing them into the riverbank. Sweepers (logs or trees lying in the water) may be a hazard.

The main current flows along the New Jersey side to the left of Quicks Island. There is a fairly narrow channel between gravel bars with standing waves to 2 feet, continuing until deflected by the New Jersey riverbank, where the channel makes a sudden right turn. Canoeists should try to stay on the inside of the turn to avoid being pushed against the bank.

At moderate water level the channel near the Pennsylvania

riverbank to the right of Quicks Island is blocked by shallows and gravel bars.

Quicks Island and Rift are named for the family of Tom Quick, the "Avenger of the Delaware." (See the features section of this chapter.)

Map 14

248.2. Crawford Branch enters, Pennsylvania side.

247.7. A Class I rapid. Scattered submerged boulders may be a hazard.

247.6. Enter Orchard Eddy, slow water continuing well past Milford.

247.3. Vandermark Creek enters, Pennsylvania side.

246.9. Sawkill Creek enters, Pennsylvania side. Sawkill Falls, one of the most spectacular cascades in the region, is on this creek about one mile from the Delaware near Grey Towers, the estate of "father of conservation" Gifford Pinchot. (See the features section of this chapter.)

246.5. Shimers Brook enters, New Jersey side.

246.2. Milford Beach Access, Milford, Pennsylvania, maintained by the National Park Service. There is ample parking, paved boat ramp, rest rooms, drinking water, telephone, picnic tables, and a swimming beach. Access from U.S. Route 209.

A concrete bridge abutment on the Pennsylvania side and its rock counterpart across the river mark the location of the old Milford Bridge, constructed of steel in 1889. The old bridge has been replaced by the modern concrete bridge slightly downstream. This is the site of Wells Ferry, which plied across the Delaware in the early nineteenth century.

There is a 20-foot-tall concrete tower standing atop the Pennsylvania bridge abutment. This is a gauging station to measure the flow of the Delaware River. According to a 1954 ruling of the United States Supreme Court, New York may draw water from the Delaware watershed (mainly from reservoirs on the East and West Branches and on the Neversink River) for consumption in New York City, as long as flow to downstream cities in New Jersey and Pennsylvania is not impaired.

The community of Milford, Pennsylvania, is about one mile from the beach. All services are available, including restaurants and groceries.

246.1. Pass under the Milford-Montague Toll Bridge, opened

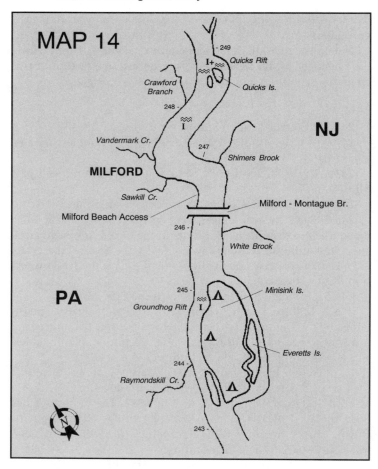

to traffic in 1953. When it was first constructed, this bridge was selected as one of the most beautiful steel bridges in the country.

245.9. White Brook enters, New Jersey side.

245.6. Camping. NPS primitive campsite, New Jersey side.

245.1. Upstream end of Minisink Island, which extends 2 miles. Minisink is the Lenape name for this area, and means "stony ground." A sizable community of Indians lived on this island when the first European settlers arrived.

The main channel runs to the right of the island, and begins with a Class I rapid known as Groundhog Rift. There are standing waves to 1¹/₂ feet and no obstructions. The left channel is passable at moderate water levels.

244.6. Everetts Island, in the channel to the left (New Jersey side) of Minisink Island.

244.3. Raymondskill Creek enters, Pennsylvania side.

243.8. A very narrow channel, passable at moderate water level, leads left from the main channel on the right side of Minisink Island. This passage rejoins the river at the downstream end of Minisink Island. There is a Class I rapid near the channel closest to the Pennsylvania side.

Camping is permitted at six NPS primitive campsites on Minisink Island.

243.4. Downstream end of Minisink Island. There is an exposed gravel bar where the channels rejoin.

Map 15

242.9. Upstream end of Namanock Island. Channels to the left and right are passable without obstructions.

Camping is permitted at four NPS primitive campsites on Namanock Island.

242.7. Conashaugh Creek enters, Pennsylvania side.

242.0. Downstream end of Namanock Island. River is slow-moving for next 1.6 miles.

241.4. Dry Creek enters, Pennsylvania side.

240.8. Camping. Sandyston camping area, New Jersey side; four NPS primitive sites, spaced about .1 mile apart; privies.

240.3. Adams Creek enters, Pennsylvania side. Moderate riffle with no obstructions.

239.1. Dingmans Creek enters, Pennsylvania side. Famous Dingmans Falls and Silver Thread Falls are on this creek about 1.5 miles from the river, accessible via Dingmans Creek Road in Dingmans Ferry.

238.7. Gravel bars and shallows on left.

238.5. Pass under Dingmans Bridge, constructed in 1900, one of the few remaining private toll bridges in America. This is the site of village of Dingmans Ferry. (See the description of Dingmans Ferry in the features section of the following chapter.)

238.4. Dingmans Ferry Access, Dingmans Ferry, Pennsylvania. Operated by the National Park Service, with plenty of parking, a wide paved boat ramp, rest rooms, telephones, and trash disposal. Access from Dingsmans Ferry road, one mile from U.S. Route 209.

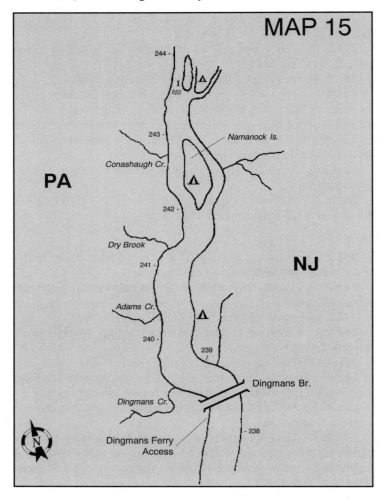

Features

Tom Quick and Indian Massacres

According to Ripley's "Believe It Or Not," Tom Quick killed more Indians after he died than the 99 he dispatched during his lifetime. Before this gruesome story may be told, some background is necessary.

When Europeans first arrived in the Delaware Valley, they encountered a sparse group of peace-loving Indians known as the

25. Dingmans Bridge, c. 1910. The scene is little changed today. Photo courtesy of the Pike County Historical Society.

Lenni Lenape. Only 8,000 to 12,000 in number, the Lenni Lenape were scattered in small communities throughout Delaware, eastern Pennsylvania, southern New Jersey, and the upper Delaware Valley. A Lenape community known as the Minsi (people of the stony country) lived in isolation from the rest of the population near what is today Milford. At first the Minsi greeted the white settlers in their traditional manner of hospitality and sharing.

William Penn, who arrived in Philadelphia in 1682, brought with him Quaker ideals. Penn practiced his belief that Indians and whites could live together in harmony. In return, the Lenape regarded Penn as their brother and held him in confidence and respect.

Unfortunately, Penn was present for only four years between 1682 and his death in 1718. Without his guidance, relations with the Indians deteriorated rapidly. The breaking point may have come in 1737, with the infamous Walking Purchase. Two of William Penn's sons convinced the reluctant Lenapes that their father had obtained a deed from the Indians in 1686 that gave the English all the lands within a day-and-a-half walk north from

Wrightstown, Bucks County. The Indians presumed this distance to be about 25 miles. The Penns, however, had other ideas. On September 19, 1737, three runners set forth from the starting point, accompanied by horses carrying provisions and two Indian observers. In the allotted day and a half, the athletes had covered 65 miles. The Indians had been cheated sorely; in the words of one Lenape observer, "He run, that's not fair, he was to walk."

Shortly after the outbreak of the French and Indian War, the Lenape aligned themselves with the French. Over the next several decades, they avenged themselves against whites of all nationalities through a campaign of scalp hunting and plunder. The atrocities, on both sides, were as severe in the Minisink, home of the Minsi, as anywhere in the Lenape nation.

One such incident involved Major Moses Van Campen of Pahaquarry. Van Campen was captured by a band of marauding Lenape in the spring of 1780. But Van Campen and two fellow captives were able to escape one night by cutting their bonds with a knife that Van Campen had secreted. Nine Indians were killed in the escape, and a tenth retreated into the woods. Before the last Indian disappeared, however, Van Campen wounded him in the shoulder with a hatchet. Many years later, in peacetime, this same Indian met Van Campen and identified himself by the hatchet scar on his back.

Another tale concerns the abduction of Sally Decker and her brother, who lived with their parents near the south end of Mashipacong Island. In 1750 the children crossed the river to tend their cows on the other side. Just when they were ready to return home, two Indians appeared out of the woods and snatched the children away. Eight years later, Sally's mother entreated a familiar Indian to help her find her daughter. The Indian said that he would try, and later that summer returned with a squaw at his side. The squaw was Sally, who had learned the ways and language of the Minsi. Sally said that her brother had married an Indian woman and had not been seen for years. After staying with her parents for a few weeks, and despite their heartrending pleas, Sally went back to the forest, her two sons, and her warrior husband, never to return.

The stage is now set for the legend of Tom Quick. Tom Quick, Sr., a Dutchman, came to the Delaware Valley in 1733. Quick was friendly with the Indians and lived on peaceful terms with them until the outbreak of the French and Indian War. Then, on a cold winter day in 1756, the elder Quick and his two sons, John and Tom, Jr., ventured across the Delaware to New Jersey to inspect their farmlands. There they were ambushed by a party of Lenape. The Quicks were unarmed and attempted to run for safety across the river. Tom Quick, Sr., old and gouty, urged his sons to go on without him. Then, as the boys retreated, the Indians fell upon the elder Quick, killed and scalped him, and took a pair of silver knee buckles from his body. Then and there Tom Quick, Jr., vowed that he would avenge his father's death by never letting any Indian escape from him alive.

Tom Quick's campaign of revenge continued until his death in 1796. He was cunning and merciless in his mission, often befriending Indians and then killing them at an opportune moment. The most famous tale has it that one day while Tom was splitting logs in a clearing, seven Indians came up to him, intent on taking him away. Tom said that he would go, but asked if the Indians would first help him split the last large log. As Tom drove a wedge deeper into the log, he instructed the Indians to pull the log apart at the split with their fingers. When the log was nearly split, Tom quickly knocked the wedge out, and the log snapped shut on the Indians' fingers. Then, at his leisure, Tom dispatched the seven, one at a time.

Another legend has it that Tom once apprehended an Indian family in a canoe. He quickly killed the mother and father, then hesitated as he approached the infant. Any thoughts of mercy were short-lived, however, for Tom said to himself, "Nits make lice," and then killed the baby with his hatchet.

Whenever Tom killed an Indian, he would search the body for his father's silver buckles. One day in a tavern he met an Indian named Mushwink, who had long ago been Tom's friend. Mushwink became quite drunk, began to brag about some of his exploits, and finally produced a pair of silver buckles exclaiming, "Me Tom Quick, me Tom Quick now." Tom grabbed a gun from over the fireplace, but the innkeeper prevented Tom from killing the Lenape in the tavern. Mushwink, realizing what he had done, walked proudly out the door; Tom shot him dead in the street.

Before Tom Quick died, his only regret was that he had not killed more Lenape. Upon his death, according to legend, gleeful Indians took pieces of Quick's body to show their brethren

that Quick was at last gone. By this demonstration many Indians were infected with smallpox and died, so Tom Quick's vengeance was carried on from his grave.

Some accounts portray Tom Quick as a hero, "the Avenger of
the Delaware." Modern authorities regard him as a psychopathic
killer. Nevertheless, stories of Tom Quick are told often in the
Delaware Valley. Many of the Quick family are buried in the old
graveyard nestled amongst the pines near the entrance to Grey
Towers. A monument to Tom Quick himself may be found at the
intersection of Broad and Sarah Streets in Milford. Interred in the
base of this monument is a glass jar containing the remains of
Tom Quick. The Tom Quick Inn is also on Broad Street, where
for many years a painting of the legendary split log could be seen
on the door.

Milford, Pennsylvania

When Abraham Lincoln was shot at Ford's Theater in 1865, his
attendants rested his head on a flag that had been hanging from
the balcony. This flag, stained with Lincoln's blood, now hangs
in a glass case at the Pike County Historical Society's museum in
Milford. Located in "The Columns" house on U.S. Route 209, the
museum contains a potpourri of items representative of earlier
life in Pike County. There are dozens of projectile points of the
Lenape and their forebears, old farm tools, early hotel registers,
items of Victorian clothing, photo albums, volumes of geneal-
ogy, and perhaps most important, a wealth of knowledge in the
members and officers of the historical society. The little museum
is reminiscent of a grandmother's attic, for although the collections are well-organized, they are crammed so tightly together
that it is difficult to tell where the arrowheads end and the farm
tools begin.

According to tradition, Milford was founded in 1733 with the
settlement of Tom Quick, Sr. The community was later known
as Wells Ferry; the origin of the modern name is not clear. Milford
has been a residential and vacation-oriented community since
the mid-nineteenth century.

Milford's most famous citizens were "Indian Slayer" Tom
Quick, "Father of Conservation" Gifford Pinchot, and philoso-
pher Charles Saunders Pierce. This heritage aside, Milford is a fascinating place. Sawkill Creek rushes through a glen immediately
south of town; the old Metz ice plant, now owned by the Na-

tional Park Service, is located in this glen on the site of an old mill. There are numerous old inns, churches, and homes about the town, each with its own history.

The physical layout of the Milford community is worthy of interest. Grassy alleyways bisect the blocks between the main residential streets, which are lined with tall shade trees and Victorian homes. The wide sidewalks on Broad Street are made of great slabs of blue slate quarried in the vicinity. Hitching posts remain at intervals throughout the community, although their utility ended decades ago.

Milford may be reached from the Delaware at the Milford Beach access. Take a short walk up the beach road to Route 209, then turn right to Harford Street.

Grey Towers

On a hill above Milford, beside the tumbling waters of Sawkill Creek, stands Grey Towers. The legacy of the science of forestry in America can be traced to these grounds. It was here in the late nineteenth century that young Gifford Pinchot became acquainted with the ways of the forest, and it was from here that Pinchot went on to become the father of American conservation.

Gifford Pinchot was born into a wealthy family in 1865. James Pinchot, Gifford's father, fervently believed that the wise use of natural resources was essential to the nation's welfare. At his suggestion, Gifford decided to become a professional forester. Scientific forestry, however, was unknown in America in the 1800s, so young Gifford studied in France. When he returned, he was the first truly professional forester in America and was quickly employed at Biltmore, the Vanderbilt family estate near Asheville, North Carolina. In 1898, Pinchot became chief of the Division of Forestry in the U.S. Department of Agriculture.

Pinchot became acquainted with Theodore Roosevelt, who was himself an ardent student of nature and admirer of the conservation principles advanced by Pinchot. When Roosevelt became president, the Division of Forestry was elevated to the U.S. Forest Service; Pinchot remained as chief of the Forest Service until 1910.

Pinchot's philosophy of conservation was guided by the principle that natural resources should be managed for the greatest good of the greatest number in the long run. But there were rivals within the growing conservation movement. Foremost among these was John Muir of California, who advocated protection and preservation of forest lands and other resources lest those remaining fall to wanton consumption. The most notable disagreement between Pinchot and Muir centered on the issue of water supply at Hetch Hetchy, California. More water was needed to fill the demands of the burgeoning population; there were plans to build a great reservoir. Muir argued that the reservoir would destroy valuable resources forever; under Pinchot's philosophy the reservoir would provide the greatest good in the long run. Ironically, the same philosophical battle has been recently fought in the very front yard of Grey Towers. Advocates of the Tocks Island Dam championed Pinchot's multiple-use concept, while preservationists claimed that valuable resources would be lost if the dam were to be built. Today, John Muir's philosophy of preservation and stewardship is evident in many programs of the National Park Service, while Gifford Pinchot's legacy of management and multiple-use guide the U.S. Forest Service.

After his 10 years with the U.S. Forest Service, Pinchot went on to become a professor at Yale. He helped found and was the first president of the Society of American Foresters. Pinchot also served two terms as governor of Pennsylvania (1923–1927 and 1931–1935) and is recalled by many as one of the great governors of that state.

In 1886 James Pinchot built a 41-room mansion on the hill in Milford. This estate, Grey Towers, was Gifford Pinchot's country home until his death in 1946. The 3,600 acres surrounding the house were managed according to Pinchot's principles. For a while, Grey Towers was also used as a training facility for Yale forestry students.

In 1963 the Pinchot family donated Grey Towers to the U.S. Forest Service, with President John F. Kennedy on hand for the dedication. The Forest Service now administers the Pinchot Institute for Conservation Studies at Grey Towers, which is dedicated to the ideals of Gifford Pinchot.

Parts of the mansion and grounds are open to the public, with daily summer tours every hour. The estate is notable as a representation of upper-class life at the turn of the century. The mansion also contains exhibits of some of Pinchot's personal collections and memorabilia.

On the opposite side of a field to the south of the mansion, a shaded trail leads to Sawkill Falls. Among the most magnificent of falls along the Pocono front, Sawkill Creek cascades into a steep, narrow chasm. The falls are located on the private property of the Pinchot family, and the area is not maintained by the Forest Service. Visitors are usually permitted to visit the falls with the understanding that private property must be respected.

Grey Towers is located in Milford about two miles from the Delaware River. Go west on Harford Street, then bear left at the "Y"; the entrance to Grey Towers is well marked, and will be found on the left.

Dingmans Ferry to Smithfield Beach

Mile 238.4 to 218.0 (20.4 miles)

Entirely within the Delaware Water Gap National Recreation Area (DWGNRA), there is a wilderness aspect to the river and valley in this section. The scenery is magnificent, and access to the river is easy. At moderate water level there are exciting, but not dangerous, rapids. It is not uncommon for many hundreds of canoeists to visit this section of the river on any summer day.

This section is among the longest, in terms of time, in the course of the river. There are a few easy rapids, but slow eddies are the rule. The long S-turn of Walpack Bend adds about three miles to the straight line distance. When the wind blows from the southwest, as it often does, vigorous paddling is required to make any headway at all. To attempt the whole reach in a single day requires considerable stamina of muscle and mind. Fortunately there are enough access points and camping areas to break up the trip or canoe only selected portions.

The river here has a character similar to the immediately preceding section. Islands are large and heavily forested, favored nesting places for many species of waterfowl and other birds. The river marks the western boundary of the Ridge and Valley geophysical province, and exposures of bedrock are seen in several locations. Kittatinny Mountain rises sharply on the New Jersey side. Many species of hawks ride the updrafts along the mountain during their autumn migration. Bird-watchers flock to the area every fall to witness this spectacle.

The river channel is filled with debris remaining from the continental glacier. The rapids, which are not very severe, tumble over glacial deposits of boulders, rather than bedrock ledges like those found at Skinners Falls or Foul Rift. Three rapids—Fiddlers Elbow, Mary and Sambo, and Depew Island—can be challenging.

U.S. Route 209 roughly parallels the river in Pennsylvania, and the historic Old Mine Road, traditionally the oldest highway in

America, approaches the river in several places on the New Jersey riverbank. There are no substantial communities on either side, and commercial services are limited. The National Park Service maintains six access areas:

Dingmans Ferry, Pennsylvania, Mile 238.4
Eshback, Pennsylvania, Mile 231.6
Bushkill, Pennsylvania, Mile 228.2
Depew, New Jersey, Mile 221.3
Poxono (Pahaquarry), New Jersey, Mile 220
Smithfield Beach, Pennsylvania, Mile 218.0.

Camping for one night only via canoe is permitted at designated primitive campsites on river islands and on the riverbanks within DWGNRA. Sites are marked by a National Park Service (NPS) camp sign. Each site has a metal fire grate, and some have privies or pit toilets, but there are no other improvements. Since there is no road access, camping is only among fellow canoeists. There is a private full-service campground just south of Dingmans Ferry.

River Guide

Map 16

238.4. Dingmans Ferry Access, Dingmans Ferry, Pennsylvania. Operated by the NPS, with plenty of parking, a wide paved boat ramp, rest rooms, telephones, and trash disposal. Access from Dingmans Ferry Road, one mile from U.S. Route 209.

Dingmans Eddy, wide and slow, continues 1.6 miles. Dingmans Eddy was a favored stopping place for timber raftsmen.

237.7. Camping. Dingmans Campground, operated as a concession under a permit from the NPS. Access from the river (very shallow) and US Route 209. Full facilities. (RR 2, Box 20, Dingmans Ferry, Pennsylvania 18328, 717-828-2266.)

237.3. A series of moderate shallow riffles across the width of the river; submerged rocks may be a hazard.

236.8. Camping. One NPS primitive campsite, Pennsylvania side.

236.5. Another easy riffle.

236.3. Channel on left presents a Class I rapids. The middle and right of river is shallow and crowded with submerged rocks streaked with paint from passing canoes. The deepest channel

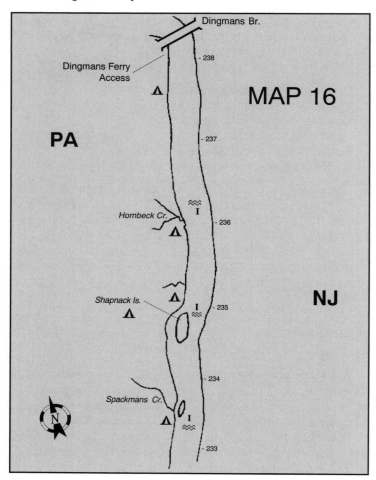

from here to Walpack Bend tends to be nearer the New Jersey bank.

236.2. Hornbeck Creek enters in a marsh, Pennsylvania side.

235.4. Easy riffle; best passage is on the left side.

235.2. Camping. Hornbeck Canoe Campsites, Pennsylvania riverbank: three NPS primitive sites, about .1 mile apart; no facilities or road access.

234.9. Shapnack Island (formerly Bacon Egg Island), a brushy gravel bar. The main channel is on the left; the channel to the right of the island is only a swampy pass through the forest.

Class I rapids; shallow, watch for submerged rocks.

Camping is permitted on Shapnack Island; one NPS primitive site.

234.4. Downstream end of Shapnack Island; another shallow riffle.

233.9. Easy riffle over shallows.

233.6. Spackmans Creek enters, Pennsylvania side, with a gravel bar near at the mouth of the creek.

There is a short Class I rapids with a deep clear channel near the New Jersey side.

Camping. Two NPS primitive campsites, Pennsylvania side, about .1 mile apart.

Map 17

233.4. The river narrows and is quite straight for the next mile. Cottages on the New Jersey bluff are among the few not razed in contemplation of the Tocks Island Dam and Reservoir. The Old Mine Road parallels the river very closely.

There is a gravel island near the New Jersey side; fast water between the island and Pennsylvania side.

232.1. Camping. One NPS primitive campsite, Pennsylvania side.

231.8. Eshback access area, Pennsylvania, maintained by NPS. Rough boat ramp, limited parking, privies, and trash disposal. Access from U.S. Route 209.

231.0. Buck Island, a broad gravel bar, in the center of the river. The right channel is marginally passable; left channel is narrower but deep enough.

230.8. Camping. An NPS primitive campsite is nestled among the trees at downstream end of Buck Island.

230.7. Toms Creek enters, Pennsylvania side.

230.6. River turns sharply left, entering Fiddlers Elbow Rift, a Class I+ rapid with no obstructions and standing waves to 2 feet. This one is fun! The deepest channel is on the right until the river bends right; then the channel is on the left. Beware whirlpools and shifting currents at the end of the rapids.

Camping. Four NPS primitive campsites, Pennsylvania side, about .1 mile apart.

229.5. Camping. Valley View Canoe Campsite, Pennsylvania riverbank: four primitive NPS campsites, no facilities or road access.

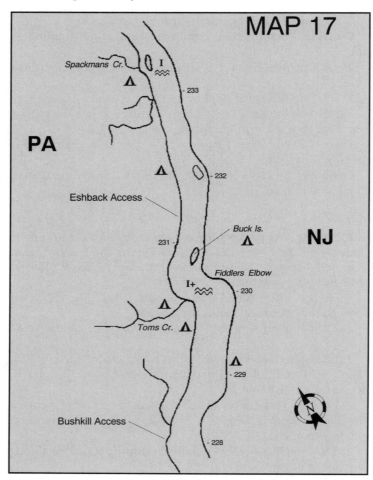

229.1. River bends slightly right in a long easy riffle; watch for submerged rocks.

Camping. Three NPS primitive campsites, New Jersey side.

228.4. U.S. Route 209 is very close to river for next .4 mile.

228.2. Bushkill access area, Bushkill, Pennsylvania, maintained by the NPS. There is a rough boat ramp, limited parking, and privies. As of 1996 the NPS was initiating substantial improvements to this access. Access from U.S. Route 209.

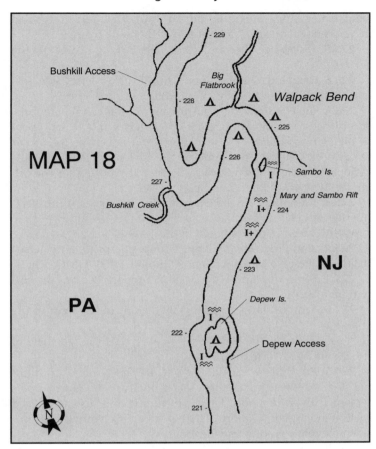

Map 18

228.0. A small gravel island is tucked near the New Jersey side. A Class I rapids, at the mouth of a creek entering from the Pennsylvania side.

227.2. Camping. Peters Canoe Campsites: several NPS primitive sites, New Jersey side.

227.0. Bush Kill enters, Pennsylvania side, with broad gravel shallows extending halfway across the river.

226.7. Begin left U-turn of Walpack Bend. Walpack Bend, a great S-turn in the Delaware, is formed where the river has cut through the hard rocks of Walpack Ridge. The bend is really a small water gap, geologically similar to the Delaware Water Gap 16 miles downstream. Rocks nearby yield many fossils.

225.8. Fast water—beware of boulders lurking just below the surface.

225.6. Camping. Quinn Canoe Campsite, New Jersey side: several NPS primitive campsites. No facilities or road access.

225.4. Big Flatbrook, "a trout stream of no mean reputation," according to Charles Hine, enters, New Jersey side. A whirlpool in Big Flatbrook near here was known to the Lenape Indians as "Wahlpeck," hence the name of the township. Alternatively, "Walpeek" means "deep water," likewise accounting for the origin of "Walpack." Take your pick.

225.3. Camping. Three NPS primitive campsites, Pennsylvania side, about .1 mile apart.

Walpack Ferry operated here in the 1800s.

225.2. Camping. River's Bend Group Campsite, New Jersey riverbank. Reservations are required; inquire at DWGNRA offices.

225.1. Begin the right U-turn out of Walpack Bend as the current increases.

224.6. Sambo Island, a small gravel bar, is in the right of the channel.

A rock slide on the New Jersey side exposes the red shale of the Bloomsburg Formation.

224.5. Enter Mary and Sambo Rift, a Class I+ rapid, continuing .6 mile, consisting of three sets of increasingly severe rapids separated by swift pools. Large protruding and just-submerged rocks may present a hazard. There is no clear channel, and considerable maneuvering may be required.

223.9. Mary and Sambo Rift ends with 2-foot standing waves and big rocks.

223.1. Camping. Hamilton Canoe Campsite, New Jersey riverbank: several NPS primitive campsites, privies, no road access.

222.8. Pass under power lines.

222.0. Upstream end of Depew Island (formerly Van Campens Island). The left passage is dry at low water levels. There is a Class I rapid in the narrow right passage, making an S-turn around the point of island; there are no obstructions, and standing waves to 2 feet. Beware being pushed against the Pennsylvania riverbank.

Depew Island is named for Nicolas Depuy, who settled in this area in 1727.

Camping. There are five NPS primitive campsites on Depew Island.

221.6. A great boulder, known as "Van Camp's Nose," protrudes from the river, Pennsylvania side.

221.4. Class I rapids at the end of Depew Island.

221.3. Depew recreation site, New Jersey, maintained by NPS. There is a dirt boat ramp, limited unimproved parking, privies, trash disposal; access from Old Mine Road.

Map 19

220.5. Begin Poxono Island (formerly Opohanough Island, then Mine House Island). At moderate water level the left channel is dry and impassable, just a brushy path through the forest. The current is swift in the main channel.

219.9. Poxono (Pahaquarry) access area, New Jersey, maintained by the National Park Service. There is a steep paved ramp, limited parking, trash disposal. Access from Old Mine Road.

220.0. River widens into Shoemakers Eddy immediately downstream of Poxono Island. Watch for motorboat traffic.

Van Campens Brook enters from behind Poxono Island, New Jersey side. A short distance up the brook is Van Campens Glen, a protected natural area where the stream cascades through a hemlock ravine. There are picnic facilities in the glen.

The Old Mine Road runs atop the New Jersey bluff.

219.7. A small gravel bar, right side of the river.

The New Jersey side of the river, marked by buoys, is reserved for unpowered craft; motorboats and Jet Skis use the Pennsylvania side. Canoes stay left! Boat wakes can sometimes be a problem to canoeists.

219.7. Mine Brook enters, New Jersey side. The abandoned adits of nineteenth-century copper mines are found a short distance up the stream. The mines are closed to public access.

219.4. Traces of a road can be seen at the river's edge on the New Jersey side. This is the site of Dimmick's Ferry, alternately known as Shoemakers Ferry, a crossing that operated in the nineteenth century.

218.0. Smithfield Beach access area, Pennsylvania, maintained by the NPS. There is a paved boat ramp, a separate canoe launch area, parking, water, rest rooms, picnicking, telephones, trash disposal, swimming beach. Access from River Road.

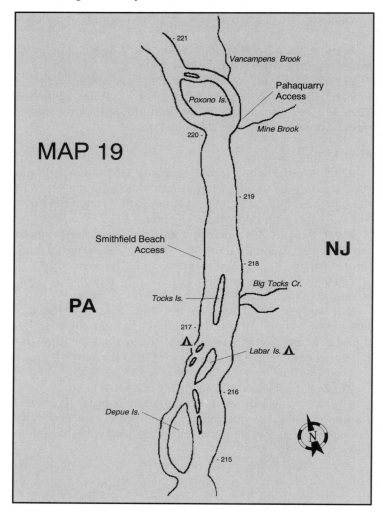

MAP 19

Features

Dingmans Ferry

It is hard to imagine that the little crossing at Dingmans Ferry was once an important gateway to westward expansion, or a favored vacation spot for the urban elite. Yet the story of Dingmans Ferry, and the ferries and bridges that spanned the Delaware River

26. Smithfield Beach (Pennsylvania), a recreation site and boat access in the Delaware Water Gap Recreation Area. The Kittatinny Ridge looms in the background. Photo by the author.

here, in many ways evokes the history of life all along this segment of the Delaware.

In 1735 Andrew Dingman, a Dutchman from Kinderhook, New York, obtained deeds to extensive lands 13 miles above Bushkill and 8 miles below Milford. The vicinity was replete with mill power from the tumbling waters of what became known as Dingmans Creek, and here Andrew Dingman chose to seek his fortune. Indeed, the homestead and environs became known as Dingmans Choice.

Dingmans Choice was in a strategic location for westbound traffic through Culvers Gap and the Old Mine Road in New Jersey. Soon after he arrived, Andrew Dingman constructed a crude raft to accommodate the growing stream of pioneers desiring to cross the river for points west. The ferry also was used to communicate and trade with the New Jersey side and, when necessary, to escape from marauding Indians. Dingman and his son Andrew II, his grandson Judge Daniel Dingman, and finally Andrew Dingman III operated the little ferry for 101 years.

By 1834 the burgeoning local population demanded a more

27. Dingmans Ferry, c. 1898, typical of the many scow ferries that plied the Delaware in the eighteenth and nineteenth centuries. The abutments of an early Dingmans Bridge stand in the background. Note the fellow fishing upstream. Photo courtesy of the Pike County Historical Society.

efficient means of crossing. Dingmans Choice and Delaware Bridge Company was chartered that year to construct and operate a bridge. A fine wooden bridge was completed in 1836 and was well used until 1847, when the spring floodwaters of the Delaware washed the bridge upriver at Milford from its piers and carried it crashing downstream into the bridge at Dingmans. Dingmans Bridge was rent into three parts; one section remained on its piers, while the other two were swept away along with the remnants of the Milford Bridge. Andrew Dingman III, who was tolltaker at the time, kept about two hundred pigeons roosting about the bridge; all were lost when the bridge was washed away. The old ferry was called back into service while plans were made to replace the bridge.

The second Dingmans Bridge was completed in 1850. It is believed that this bridge was covered, for the diaries of residents tell of hauling snow into the bridge to make for better passage by horse-drawn sleds. Unfortunately, this bridge too was short-lived. About five years after its completion, a great gale lifted the bridge wholly from its stone foundations and then dropped it into the river. Once again the ferry was hauled out of storage and put into service.

In 1856 a third wooden bridge was constructed on the existing stone piers. Evidently this bridge was poorly constructed or was made from inferior materials, for the structure collapsed and fell into the river in 1862.

Still again the ancient ferry was hauled out to ply the water between Pennsylvania and New Jersey. Until 1875 Andrew Dingman III pulled a 12-foot by 45-foot craft back and forth by an overhead cable. Then the operation was purchased by John W. Killsby who, with his son, operated the ferry until 1900. The ferry was in service 24 hours a day and could be summoned by tolling a bell from the opposite shore.

Nevertheless, the old slow ferry did not match the quickening pace of the times. In 1889, Dingmans Choice and Delaware Bridge Company sought to raise $15,000 to build a new bridge, but this effort was not successful. At about this time Dr. J. N. Miller, a Layton physician, avoided ferry delays by pulling himself across the river in a basket suspended from the ferry cable. Dingmans Choice and Delaware Bridge Company, nearly bankrupt, lost the bridge franchise at a tax sale to the Perkins brothers, owners of the Horsehead Bridge Company. The Perkins brothers were in possession of the remnants of a bridge that had crossed the Susquehanna River at Muncie. They hauled three wrought-iron trusses from that bridge to Dingmans. New stone piers were built, and the existing abutments raised six feet. The bridge was opened for traffic in 1900, with tolls assessed as follows:

2 horse wagon	25 cents
1 horse wagon	18 cents
horseless carriage	40 cents
horse and rider	10 cents
horse sled	6 cents
footman	2 cents
bicycle	5 cents
tandem	6 cents
cattle	23 cents

The bridge remains in use today, although the toll for a horseless carriage has been raised to 75 cents.

As a center of traffic and commerce, Dingmans Choice natu-
rally developed into a thriving community. By the 1840s there
were numerous dwellings, a school, store, blacksmith shop, and
at least one tavern. Dingmans Choice was famous among river
raftsmen for its accommodations, and was a favorite stopping
place. By the mid-nineteenth century the village had become
identified with the ferry operation, and in 1868, by action of the
U.S. Post Office, became officially known as Dingmans Ferry. In
the later decades of the 1800s Dingmans was a favorite place of
artists and vacationers. At least half a dozen hotels thrived during this era. One summer resident was moved to record his feel-
ings for the place in verse:

> I have journeyed far, both east and west,
> Far north and south, too, very.
> But the sweetest place amongst all the rest
> Is hill-bound Dingmans Ferry.
>
> The days I've spent among the hills
> Were joyous, free and merry,
> Amongst veteran rocks and murmuring hills,
> Found but at Dingmans Ferry.

All of the old bridges across this part of the Delaware River
were once privately owned. But candidates for local office made
political hay out of the tolls; in 1906 Alfred Marbin became the
first Republican elected to the state legislature from Pike County
in one hundred years, running on a platform of free bridges. Today, Dingman's Bridge is the only private bridge across the Delaware, and one of the last in the country. Dingmans Choice and
Delaware Bridge Company, originally chartered in 1834, continues to accommodate travellers across the Delaware between New
Jersey and Pennsylvania.

Virtually nothing remains of the village of Dingmans Ferry.
The great stone house of Andrew Dingman II, built in 1803, now
vacant and boarded up, stands sentinel at the Pennsylvania end
of the bridge. At the whitewashed wooden tollhouse is a bulle-
tin board where notices of antique shows, church fairs, and community activities are posted. Kittatinny Canoes operates a base
behind the old Dingman house, and the National Park Service
maintains a large river access just downstream from the bridge.

Old Mine Road

Along the way from Dingmans Ferry to Walpack Bend, canoeists occasionally may see a lone car driving along a road atop the bluff on the New Jersey side. The car makes slow progress, bumping and dipping through potholes, leaving a cloud of dust in its wake. "What a terrible road!" one may think. A scramble up the bank confirms this impression.

But this rugged road has survived a long time. It was here before any summer cottages, before the canals to the north and south, before rafts loaded with timber were floated to Philadelphia, before the formation of the United States, before the colonies were ruled by the King of England, before any other road of its length existed in North America. This narrow, potholed, dusty road, known as the Old Mine Road, is traditionally considered the oldest highway in America.

Legend has it that the road was used by early Dutch settlers to haul copper ore from mines near the Delaware Water Gap one hundred miles north to Kingston on the Hudson River. Although not proving that the Dutch mined copper at Pahaquarry or built the Old Mine Road, there are records indicating that Dutch explorers hunted for minerals in the Minisink as early as 1626. In 1730, two pioneers from Philadelphia tramped through the wilderness to investigate rumors of a settlement and mines far upriver. They found at Pahaquarry a thriving and long-established community. In 1787, when the first mines had been long abandoned, one investigator inquired of an aged resident about the origin of the mines and road. The old man could tell only of legends and traditions, but it was presumed that the grandfathers of his compatriots were the original settlers.

Because the Old Mine Road was a major commercial thoroughfare, communities, farms, and inns rose up along it. Generations lived and died near the road. Battles were fought in its environs. Merchants, artists, soldiers, adventurers all passed along the road and played a role in its colorful history.

For the modern-day adventurer who leaves his canoe at the river's edge, a stroll along some segments of the Old Mine Road is like a trip back through time. It is easy to imagine that the environs of the Old Mine Road are little changed in over three hundred years. Fields stand in corn just as they might have long ago. Some of the aged structures remain. Only the sounds of birds and the river penetrate the quiet; the scent of wild strawberry, rhododendron, and corn permeates the air.

There are several good places for a canoeist to explore the Old Mine Road. The first is at Mile 233.5, about one mile below Shapnack Island. This is where the summer cottages are clustered. About a mile downstream from here the road takes a very sharp left turn to a vista of a brook running through pastures and under a tiny bridge. A little further beyond, the road merges with the "Walpack Loop," a section of the Old Mine Road brought up to modern standards.

The walk upstream from Mile 233.5 is the most interesting of all. The cottages are soon left behind, and the left of the road opens into extensive cornfields. In 1760 this was the farm of one John Symmes. To the right stands a magnificent stone house, recently restored by the National Park Service. This sturdy structure was built in 1742 by Isaac Van Campen. It is reputed that the last black slave in New Jersey, named Caesar, was owned by the residents of this home when slavery was abolished in New Jersey in 1829. General Horatio Gates stayed here during his service in the American Revolution, as did Congressman (later President) John Adams on his travels between Boston and Washington.

A little farther up the road, about a mile from the starting point, is a bronze plaque and a miniature American flag, placed by the American Legion to commemorate some long-ago veteran. Behind the tree and plaque a rough trail leads steeply up into the forest. Only a hundred yards up this trail a dozen ancient tombstones are scattered on the hillside. The trees growing among the graves must be well over a hundred years old. The most prominent stone clearly marks the burial of Anna Symmes, mother-in-law of President William Henry Harrison, in 1776. Most of the other stones are very rough and illegible or unmarked.

Another good place to explore the Old Mine Road begins at Mile 230, a little below Fiddlers Elbow Rift. A short walk upstream provides a fine overlook of the rift and canoeists making their way through it. About a mile downstream on the road, to the right, a bronze plaque set in granite tells the history of the Old Mine Road. A little further is the tiny community of Flatbrook-ville. When Charles Hine explored the road in 1909, he commented that Flatbrookville had "a back-woods flavor that immediately appeals." Then there was a mill, an inn, and a store. Today the backwoods flavor is even more pronounced. Some of the buildings have been razed, and only a few houses and barns remain. It is a place whose time has passed.

The Old Mine Road closely approaches the river again at Mile 220, at Shoemakers Eddy by Poxono Island. This part of the road is more heavily traveled since it is the main way through the Delaware Water Gap National Recreation Area, but nevertheless rural charm prevails. A few hundred yards downstream a broad trail leads left alongside a stream called Mine Brook. Not far up this trail are the abandoned copper mines of several generations of prospectors. There is not much copper to be found here, and it is doubtful that any of the mines were ever commercially successful.

On a flat area between the road and river, a bit further down, is the Old Copper Mine Inn, formerly known as Shoemaker's Union Hotel. Henry Shoemaker, a soldier of the Revolution, built a large stone house on the hillside, but this house evidently has fallen beneath the Corps of Engineers' bulldozer.

From this point all the way to the Delaware Water Gap, the road is never far from the river; though improved, it is a delight for walking and exploring and likely to reveal glimpses of its long history to the careful observer.

American Indian Artifacts

Much can be told about a culture by digging through its garbage, and the garbage of aboriginal residents is abundant in the Upper Delaware Valley. Recent examination of the residue of these native peoples has allowed archaeologists to reconstruct their lifestyle.

It is not at all unusual to find an arrowhead or some other stone artifact along the banks of the Delaware. For a trained archaeologist, however, every arrowhead, or more correctly "projectile point," says something about the people who fashioned it and used it. Just as the technology and style of today's civilization differ from that of times past, so too the technology and style of Native American artifacts are indicative of the period in which they were used. By examination and correlation of many artifacts found scattered along the Upper Delaware Valley and by intense excavation and study of places where American Indians once lived, archaeologists have determined that several separate and distinct cultures lived in the area.

When construction of the Tocks Island Dam was imminent, the Department of Interior commissioned explorations for evidence of early aboriginal habitation. Dr. Herbert Kraft of Seton Hall University, a frequent lecturer on the Upper Delaware Valley, led the excavation of sites at Harry's Farm (in the vicinity of Tocks Island) and at the Philhower-Bell site near Minisink Island. It seems that these areas were attractive to ancient people for the same reasons that they are attractive today. At Harry's Farm, a spring provides water for people and small animals. The site is high enough above the river to be safe from floods, but near enough for good fishing and canoe access. There is plenty of firewood in the forest, and wild game—deer, waterfowl, and small animals—are abundant. Black bear and elk were once included among the game animals.

The first people in the Delaware Valley, Paleo-Indians, came soon after the glacier retreated. Evidence of these ancient inhabitants is scant, but has been found in the form of fluted projectile points at Pahaquarry. It has been suggested that these people included the great woolly mammoth on their menu. Mammoths were no doubt present in the area at about the same time, for their remains have been found in several places in New Jersey. There seems to be, however, no direct evidence that mammoths were hunted as game.

At the Harry's Farm excavation, 90 inches below the ground surface, archaeologists have unearthed artifacts and features left by people of the valley in a period known as the Early Archaic, which occurred as long ago as 7000 B.C. Net sinkers, choppers, anvil stones, firepits and hearths, and a single projectile fragment reveal the presence of the ancient inhabitants. Sometime during the Early Archaic period the Delaware River rose in a great flood, for a layer of sand and silt a foot thick is found overlaying some of the earliest artifacts.

In the Middle Archaic period, around 3900 B.C., there appears to have been a culture distinct from earlier and later peoples. This "Kittatinny" culture is revealed in slate knives, hammer stones, milling stones, and a distinct variety of projectile points known as "Kittatinny points."

Yet another culture was present in the Delaware Valley during the Late Archaic period, as long ago as 2600 B.C. These people utilized "Poplar Island" and "Lackawaxen" projectile points, which are characterized by elongated narrow blades. Abundant evidence of this culture was found at Harry's Farm site in the form of net sinkers, knives, drills, formed pebble tools, and numerous projectile points. A long transitional phase followed the Late Archaic period.

By A.D. 200 a culture known as "Woodland" had developed in the Upper Delaware Valley. The Woodland period was divided into two main cultures: Early to Middle Woodland and Late Woodland. Dr. Kraft has identified two distinct cultures of the Late Woodland: the Pahaquarra and the Minisink.

Clay pottery in the form of pots, bowls, cups, and flasks was widely used in the Early to Middle Woodland culture. The changing style and decoration of pottery may be used as an index of time throughout the remaining American Indian habitation. Pottery of similar characteristics was used at corresponding times over a wide geographic area, and in fact may be correlated to aboriginal groups in New York state, southern Canada, and the Ohio Valley.

Of all the Native Americans who inhabited the upper Delaware Valley, most is known of the most recent, the Late Woodland Minisink culture. These people called themselves Lenni Lenape and were known to settlers as the Delaware Indians. American Indians of the Minisink disposed of their trash in refuse pits and stored their goods in lined holes in the ground. Today these pits are a bonanza for archaeologists, for they contain the remains of the everyday lives of their users. At Harry's Farm site numerous pits have been unearthed, ranging from shallow dishes to silo-shaped pits 60 inches deep. Abundant pottery shards, occasionally an intact clay bowl or pot, food remains, tools and implements, ornaments, and other clues to Minisink life have been found.

Archaeologists working at Harry's Farm site also have discovered postmolds (the imprint and residue of wooden posts in the ground) in patterns revealing the shape and structure of native homes. These "long houses" were constructed by sticking saplings into the ground 2 to 3 feet apart along the edge of an oval up to 62 feet long and 22 feet wide. The saplings were bent toward the center and then joined at the top. Horizontal members were lashed along the side like a trellis, and shingles made of elm, linden, and/or chestnut bark were attached. Each long house contained a firepit, storage pits inside and nearby, and up to three rooms. At least four such houses were discovered at the site of Harry's Farm.

Archaeologists have been most excited by the discovery of Indian skeletons buried in shallow graves or in storage pits. Many such burials were found near Minisink Island, several at Harry's Farm site, and at least one near Dingmans Bridge. Most of the skeletons were found facing toward the west. The Lenape Indians believed, to borrow the words of Herbert Kraft, that "the sun and everything else goes toward the west, even the dead when they die," and that "the land of the spirits lies in the southwest, in the country of good hunting."

From the clues discovered by archaeologists and from the observations of the earliest pioneers and missionaries, it seems that the aboriginal inhabitants of the Upper Delaware Valley lived in family groups, not villages, about one mile apart throughout the valley. They subsisted by hunting, gathering, fishing, and gardening. They were evidently a peaceful group, for there is no evidence that their homes were fortified or built in a defensive manner. They hunted primarily with wooden bows and arrows tipped by stone points, and fished for the shad and eels that migrated, and still migrate, in the Delaware River. They gardened with crude stone hoes and cooked their meals in ornamented clay pots. The Lenape probably canoed the Delaware in hollow chestnut logs. The growing population of white settlers forced the Lenape north to Ontario and west to Ohio and Oklahoma in the early nineteenth century. Their descendants remain there to this day.

Modern canoeists and other visitors to the Delaware Valley will find collections of American Indian artifacts at the High Point State Park office in New Jersey (on Route 23 at the crest of Kittatinny Ridge, four miles south of Port Jervis) and at the Pike County Historical Society Museum in Milford. Kraft and other archaeologists occasionally lecture at state and national park facilities in the area.

Federal law now prohibits removal of American Indian artifacts. Any find should be reported to the National Park Service—it could be an important clue in the interpretation of early life in the Delaware Valley.

The Tocks Island Dam

Strictly from a canoeist's standpoint, Tocks Island is of minor interest; there are several excellent campsites found on the middle and downstream end of the island, and mild riffles gurgle on both sides. From a broader point of view, however, this sliver of land six miles upstream from the Delaware Water Gap is the focus of the greatest controversy ever raised concerning use of the Delaware.

In response to the devastating flood of 1955, the Delaware River Basin Commission, in cooperation with the U.S. Army Corps of Engineers, proposed that a great dam be built at Tocks Island to impede floodwaters. This dam would also be used to store water for consumption, provide hydroelectric power, augment low flow to prevent saltwater from moving too far upstream (to Philadelphia's water supply intakes), and to provide recreation. The Tocks Island Dam was to be 160 feet high, stretching between the Kittatinny Ridge in New Jersey and the Pocono front in Pennsylvania. Water would be impounded in a reservoir extending 37 miles to Port Jervis.

Almost as soon as the Tocks Island proposal was announced in 1962, local residents (many of whom would have to leave, as their homes would be inundated) and the budding environmental movement voiced their opposition.

The U.S. Congress appropriated money to acquire land that would be inundated by the great reservoir. As acquisition proceeded, there were many ugly confrontations between the Army Corps of Engineers and local residents. In some cases, squatters moved into homes that the owners had been forced to leave. These squatters used local services and enrolled their children in local schools, but paid no property taxes. The government, local property owners, and squatters all opposed each other, and conflicts intensified. Eventually the Corps of Engineers bulldozed and burned several houses as the squatters ran into the forest, shouting oaths of vengeance. Many abandoned houses, or their foundations, remain to this day in the area that was to be flooded.

Meanwhile, a law was enacted requiring that an environmental impact study be made of every proposed federal project. When the environmental impact study was finally completed for the Tocks Island Dam, it showed that the environmentalists' claims had merit. The dam and reservoir would flood valuable natural, recreational, and historical resources. Moreover, the water level in the reservoir would fluctuate radically, leaving mud flats along the edges. In time, debris, silt, and vegetation would fill the reservoir. Most important for canoeists, the dam would erase 37 miles of gorgeous river travel and replace it with a flat lake criss-crossed by motorboats.

The Tocks Island dilemma had become highly visible to the public by the early 1970s. There was political pressure—both ways—to take action. Advocates of construction lobbied in Trenton and other state capitals. A resident near Walpack on the Old Mine Road, voicing the sentiments of many locals, posted a huge sign: "The Lord Giveth, and the Government Taketh Away." Environmental groups took Tocks Island as a cause celebre and demonstrated their views at every opportunity. The DRBC was pressed to make a final decision.

In the summer of 1974, New Jersey Governor Brendan Byrne announced that he would personally inspect, by canoe, the site of the proposed dam. Many government officials and others involved in the controversy were invited to participate. To prepare for the event, the Youth Conservation Corps (YCC) from Stokes State Forest, New Jersey, was commissioned to clean up Tocks Island itself, where the governor was to make a speech. Five dumptruck loads of garbage, including old tires and a kitchen sink, were ferried by canoe off the island.

Kittatinny Canoes donated the use of about 40 canoes for Byrne's expedition. The athletic governor took the bow seat in one, accompanied by a state trooper and a 17-year-old girl from the YCC. Then the rest of the party—dignitaries, reporters, onlookers—paddled out. At least a hundred craft were included in the flotilla as demonstrators and day paddlers joined in. Byrne completed the journey with a short speech at Tocks Island amid a throng of demonstrators carrying signs like "Doom the Dam."

Over the course of the following year the governors of the four DRBC states commissioned studies, prepared reports, and conducted evaluations. But by August 1975 no final decision on Tocks Island had been reached. Governor Milton Shapp of Pennsylvania was firmly in favor of the dam. Governor Hugh Carey of New York was firmly opposed. Governor Trippett of Delaware said he would vote as New Jersey did. And New Jersey's Governor Byrne remained undecided.

Most of the responsibility in New Jersey for evaluating the dam proposal and for recommending a decision lay with David J. Bardin, Byrne's Commissioner of Environmental Protection. Bardin, of course, had studied the reports and listened to the arguments about the Tocks Island Dam. But still he was not ready to make his recommendation to the governor. Beyond the dry studies and evaluations, Bardin wanted to include his personal impressions of Tocks in the decision-making process. So he planned a private visit to the scene to gain better firsthand knowledge.

Accompanied only by three guides from the YCC, Bardin hiked the Appalachian Trail from the Delaware Water Gap to Millbrook Road, a distance of 12 miles. At certain places the river could be seen clearly from the ridgetop trail, and Bardin saw hundreds of canoes making their way through the rapids and eddies. As he hiked through the afternoon, Bardin spoke with many of the other hikers he encountered. He asked them about their hometowns, about what drew them to the trail that day, and about their thoughts on the dam. Almost all the hikers knew of the Tocks Island proposal, and almost all were opposed to it.

Finally, near the trailhead at Millbrook Road, Bardin took out his pen to sign the trail register. He looked over the roster of hikers, their points of origin, and their destinations. Then, as he signed the register, Bardin commented that he would use the same pen to sign his recommendation to the governor—in opposition of the dam.

The following week the DRBC met to decide the fate of the Tocks Island Dam project. Only Governor Shapp voted in favor. The dam was defeated. No more money was appropriated. Finally, on December 15, 1993, authorization for the Tocks Island Dam was rescinded. The Delaware will remain a free-flowing river.

Smithfield Beach to Martins Creek

Mile 218.0 to 194.2 (23.8 miles)

The famous Delaware Water Gap and the severe rapids at Foul Rift dominate this section. This section begins as the previous section ended, with the river defining the boundary between the Pocono Mountains to the west and the Kittatinny Ridge to the east. At the water gap the river has gouged a 1,300-foot-deep cleft in Kittatinny Ridge. At Manunka Chunk the river meanders through the terminal moraine of the continental glacier. Below the moraine the river drops 22 feet over the sharp limestone ledges at Foul Rift, one of the most hazardous rapids on the Delaware.

Above the water gap the river is characterized by boulder rapids separated by shallow pools. Below the gap, however, the rapids fall more severely over ledges, and the pools are much deeper. The water is 55 feet deep just below the gap; next to Big Eddy at Narrowsburg, this is the deepest point on the river. It is 18 feet deep at Portland, 30 feet deep at Belvidere, and 42 feet deep below Foul Rift.

The Delaware Water Gap marks another change in the river. Forests and little villages predominate upstream from the water gap, while below the gap the river enters more densely populated areas. The forests give way to cleared farmland, and here and there industrial centers rise from the riverbanks. There are huge cement plants at Portland, chemical refineries at Belvidere, and two giant power stations, one at Martins Creek, the other at Portland. Above the water gap the rustic Old Mine Road parallels the river on the New Jersey side. However, below the gap Interstate Route 80 (I-80) crosses the river and runs nearby for five miles. U.S. Route 46 continues along the New Jersey bank between Columbia and Belvidere. Recreation on the river below the water gap becomes more motor-oriented; there may be many power boats, Jet Skis, and pontoon boats. Homes and vacation cottages line the riverbanks in most areas.

28. Reminiscent of a Roman aqueduct, the Erie-Lackawanna Railroad crosses the river just downstream from the Delaware Water Gap. Photo by the author.

The first 10 miles of this section are within the Delaware Water Gap National Recreation Area (DWGNRA) and Middle Delaware National Scenic and Recreational River, part of the National Park system. The National Park Service (NPS) has several activities and exhibits accessible to canoeists. The Appalachian Trial, a continuous footpath between Georgia and Maine, crosses the Delaware River on the I-80 bridge.

There are six public access areas in this section:

Smithfield Beach, Pennsylvania, Mile 218.0
Worthington State Forest, New Jersey, Mile 214.7
Kittatinny Point, New Jersey, Mile 211.7
Portland, Pennsylvania, Mile 207.6
Portland Station, Pennsylvania, Mile 206.7
Martins Creek, Pennsylvania, Mile 194.2.

Camping for one night only via canoe is permitted at designated primitive campsites on river islands and on the riverbanks within DWGNRA. Sites are marked by a NPS camp sign. Each site has a metal fire grate, but there are no other improvements—no picnic tables, or privies—so be prepared to rough it. Since there is no road access, camping is only among fellow canoeists. Camping is also permitted at Worthington State Forest, and at several private campgrounds.

River Guide

Map 20

218.0. Smithfield Beach access area, Pennsylvania, maintained by the NPS. There is a paved boat ramp, a separate canoe launch area, parking, water, rest rooms, picnicking, telephones, trash disposal, swimming beach. Access from River Road.

217.9. Upstream end of Tocks Island. Channels on either side are passable with swift current and short riffles, though the left channel is narrower. The Old Mine Road runs very close atop the New Jersey riverbank.

217.1. Downstream end of Tocks Island. This is the site of the proposed Tocks Island Dam. (See the features section of the previous chapter.) A slight riffle runs from the channels on both sides of the island.

217.2. Big Tocks and Little Tocks Creeks enter, New Jersey side.

217.0. Pass under a high-tension line, with a clear cut through the forest on the New Jersey side.

216.8. Two small islands are nestled against the Pennsylvania side.

Camping. One NPS primitive campsite, Pennsylvania side.

216.7. Upstream end of Labar Island. Channels to the left and right are passable without obstructions.

Camping. NPS primitive campsite, on Labar Island.

216.1. Downstream end of Labar Island.

The Hiaheah Picnic Area, maintained by the NPS, is atop the Pennsylvania riverbank. Watch for the red brick foundations of razed cottages. There are picnic tables and privies. Although the riverbank is very steep and not suitable for canoe launch from the road, canoeists can scramble up the riverbank to the picnic area.

216.0. Upstream end of Woodcock Bar, a slender island extending diagonally downstream. The main channel is on the left, with shallows and exposed gravel bars. The channel to the right is passable, though at low water the entrance to it is nearly blocked by gravel bars.

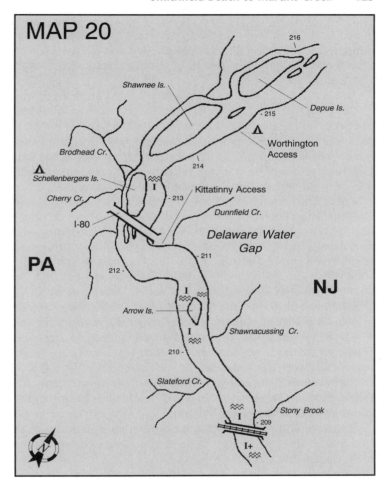

MAP 20

216

Shawnee Is.

Depue Is.

215

Worthington
Access

Brodhead Cr.

214

Schellenbergers Is.

Cherry Cr.

213

Kittatinny Access

Dunnfield Cr.

I-80

Delaware Water
Gap

211

PA

212

NJ

Arrow Is.

Shawnacussing Cr.

210

Slateford Cr.

Stony Brook

209

I+

215.9. Upstream end of Depue Island, in the right channel be-hind Woodcock Bar. Depue Island extends one mile downstream against the Pennsylvania side. The main channel is to the left, but the narrow right channel is passable. Depue Island is private— no trespassing.

215.5. Worthington State Forest campground is situated atop the bluffs on the New Jersey riverbank; camper registration is at the forest office at the Worthington access area, one mile down-stream.

214.7. Downstream end of Depue Island.

214.6. Worthington State Forest access area, New Jersey, maintained by the New Jersey State Park Service. There is a paved boat ramp, rest rooms, trash disposal, telephones, and fresh water. The state forest office is a few feet from the boat ramp. Access from Old Mine Road.

This is the site of Walkers Ferry, a nineteenth-century crossing.

Camping. Worthington State Forest (New Jersey) has about 80 campsites on the river's edge between Mile 215.5 and Mile 214.5. Each site has a picnic table and fireplace with drinking water nearby. Group campsites are also available. It must be noted that Worthington State Forest is very popular with "car campers," and it is often difficult to find an available site on weekends.

214.5. Shawnee Point, between Depue Island upstream and Shawnee Island downstream, is on the Pennsylvania side opposite the Worthington access. The Shawnee Inn, white with a red roof, stands near the point. Shawnee Inn is the last of the great resort hotels on the Delaware River. Vacation havens at the Delaware Water Gap and at Shohola disappeared decades ago, but the Shawnee Inn has kept up with the times. Developed by C. C. Worthington in 1910 as the Buckwood Inn, the Shawnee became known as one of the finest golf resorts in the country. In the 1940s the property was taken over by Fred Waring, the big band "Pennsylvanian." The Shawnee Inn today is a complete resort community, with the 100-room inn, private cottages, time-shared condominiums, swimming, nightclub entertainment, and the Delaware River. The famous Shawnee Playhouse is nearby in the community of Shawnee-on-Delaware.

Upstream end of Muskrat Island on the left side of the river. Channel to the left is clear. There is a moderate current in the main channel on the right.

Upstream end of Shawnee Island (formerly Van Campens Island), which extends 1.2 miles along the Pennsylvania side. The main flow of the river runs between the New Jersey side and the island, but the narrow channel between Shawnee Island and the Pennsylvania side is passable. The second and seventeenth holes of the famous Shawnee Resort Golf Course cross the channel shortly after its entrance. The channel bottom is usually littered with golf balls. Golf balls carried by the current are often seen on the river bottom well below the water gap. Shawnee Island is privately owned—no trespassing.

213.4. Downstream end of Shawnee Island.

213.3. Pass under power line marked by red balls.

213.1. Two stone abutments on the New Jersey riverbank are all that remain of the old Lackawanna Railroad Bridge, which washed away in the double hurricane flood of 1955.

Brodhead Creek enters, Pennsylvania side. The creek has built gravel bars that extend two-thirds of the way across the river. Thirty-seven campers at Camp Davis, on Brodhead Creek in Stroudsburg, were drowned during the 1955 flood.

Ledges on the New Jersey side are covered with graffiti.

Upstream end of Schellenbergers Island. The channel on the Pennsylvania side is dry at moderate water level. A branch of Brodhead Creek enters the channel slightly downstream.

212.9. A Class I rapid with standing waves to 1½ feet near the New Jersey side.

Cherry Creek enters, Pennsylvania side, to channel right of Schellenbergers Island.

212.7. Camping. Two NPS primitive campsites on Schellenbergers Island.

212.5. Gap Islands on the right side of the river. Channels on the right are passable at moderate water level.

212.4. A Class I rapid is in the main channel near the New Jersey side, with standing waves to 1½ feet and no obstructions.

212.2. Pass under the Delaware Water Gap Toll Bridge, completed in 1953 and carrying I-80. The Appalachian Trail, extending from Georgia to Maine, crosses this bridge. (See the features section of this chapter.)

212.1. The river bends sharply left, entering the famous Delaware Water Gap. (See description in the features section of this chapter.) Hemlock woods cover the steep slopes of Mt. Minsi (elevation 1,461 ft.) on Pennsylvania side. After a rain, runoff tumbles down Mt. Minsi via several waterfalls.

Resort Point overlook, a roadside (Route 611) scenic view atop the Pennsylvania riverbank, maintained by the NPS. This is the site of the Kittatinny House, a lavish 1800s resort hotel.

211.7. Kittatinny access area, New Jersey, maintained by the NPS. There is a sand beach with a corduroy boat ramp. This is one of the busiest access areas anywhere on the river. The Kittatinny Point Visitor Center of the DWGNRA is at the top of the bluff above the beach. There are rest rooms, fresh water, and shaded picnic tables. Information about activities in the recreation area is available here. (For further details, see the features section of this chapter.)

211.5. Dunnfield Creek enters, New Jersey side. The rock profile of an Indian, with forest headdress, can be seen on the cliffs of Mt. Tammany (elevation 1,549 ft.), New Jersey side.

211.0. Steep cliffs and landslides on both sides.

210.9. Point of Gap overlook, a roadside (Route 611) scenic view atop the Pennsylvania riverbank. Maintained by the NPS. Hiking trails lead up Mt. Minsi.

210.8. Upstream end of Arrow Island.

The channel on the New Jersey side is narrow, beginning with a Class I+ rapid with big standing waves. At low water the Pennsylvania channel may be nearly blocked by shallows.

210.6. Downstream end of Arrow Island. Rocky ledges extend from Pennsylvania side. There are numerous protruding and barely submerged boulders on the left for the next .2 mile.

Arrow Island overlook, a roadside (Route 611) scenic view, atop the Pennsylvania riverbank. Maintained by the NPS. There is no access from the river.

210.1. Shawnacussing Creek enters, New Jersey side.

209.5. Slateford Creek enters, Pennsylvania side. A small gravel bar extends into river.

The confluence of Slateford Creek marks the southern boundary of the DWGNRA. National Park Service jurisdiction ends here. Downstream from this point the lands adjacent to the river and river islands are mostly privately owned.

209.4. Site of Deckers Ferry, another nineteenth-century crossing.

209.0. Stony Brook enters, New Jersey side, with a gravel bar extending .1 mile downstream.

At one time there were slate quarries in operation on both sides of the river; a historic quarry can be visited at Slateford Farm in the DWGNRA.

Current increases over boulders and shallows to a Class I rapid, then passes under the compound arches of the Erie-Lackawanna Railroad Bridge. Immediately under the bridge a Class I+ rapid flows from left to right with a few boulders. Standing waves to 2 feet continue downstream .1 mile.

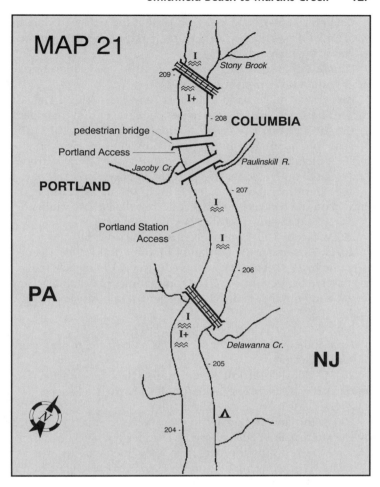

Map 21

207.6. Portland Access, Pennsylvania, on land of the Delaware River Joint Bridge Commission, immediately under the pedestrian bridge. There is a steep asphalt ramp and trash barrel, but no other facilities and no designated parking area. Although heavily used by commercial river outfitters, the access area is not maintained. The Town of Portland plans to establish a park and canoe launch at this site.

Columbia access, New Jersey, on land of the Village of Columbia. Dirt landing area, no facilities, no parking. The area is posted as for use by village residents only.

Lunch: Portland Diner, 100 yds. south of pedestrian bridge from Portland (Pennsylvania) access.

Pass under the Portland-Columbia Pedestrian Bridge. The last covered bridge to span the Delaware was washed from these piers in the 1955 flood. The original bridge was built in 1839. The present four-span steel bridge was completed in 1958 on the original piers and abutments, and is open only to pedestrians. The original bridge house stands at the Pennsylvania end of the bridge. Elevation above sea level, from 287 to 295 feet, is indicated on the concrete bridge pier nearest the Pennsylvania side.

An 1874 map shows a Dills Ferry crossing here.

207.4. Jacoby Creek enters, Pennsylvania side.

207.3. Pass under the Portland-Columbia Toll Bridge, opened to traffic in 1953. This bridge was constructed to replace the aging covered bridge upstream. The communities of Columbia, New Jersey, and Portland, Pennsylvania, stand at opposite ends of the bridge.

A moderate riffle begins under the bridge.

Limestone quarried in the vicinity is used in the manufacture of Portland cement.

207.1. The Paulinskill River enters, New Jersey side. The Paulinskill was known as Tockhockonetcunk to the Lenape.

206.9. Class I rapids, no obstructions.

206.7. Portland Station access area, Pennsylvania, maintained by the Metropolitan Edison Electric Company. Gravel boat ramp, parking, trash disposal, privies, and a few picnic tables. The access gate is locked at night, and no overnight parking or camping is permitted. Access from River Road 1 mile south of Portland, Pennsylvania.

206.4. A Class I rapid with a few protruding boulders.

206.3. Pass under power lines.

206.2. The Metropolitan Edison power plant, with two high smokestacks, stands on the Pennsylvania riverbank. A concrete cooling water outfall extends into the middle of the river—stay clear.

206.0. A substantial but unnamed creek enters, Pennsylvania side.

205.4. Pass under the five-span bridge of the old Delaware,

Lackawanna, and Western Railroad. There is a small gravel island on the left side of the river just below the bridge.

An unnamed creek enters, Pennsylvania side.

205.3. A Class I rapid with standing waves to 1½ feet flows along the Pennsylvania side. The left three-quarters of the river is very shallow.

Eagles Nest, a private camp, is on the New Jersey riverbank.

205.1. Delawanna Creek, New Jersey side.

205.2. Rapids increase in severity (to Class I+) along the Pennsylvania side. Be wary of a few just-submerged boulders.

204.9. Enters Anters Eddy, slow water continuing 2.5 miles downstream.

204.1. Camping. Delaware River Campgrounds, Ramseyburg, New Jersey. A private campground with tent sites accessible from the river, all facilities. Access from New Jersey Route 46.

204.0. The little community of Ramseyburg, New Jersey, is on the left.

203.2. Camping. Driftstone on the Delaware, Mt. Bethel, Pennsylvania. A private campground offering tent sites with access from the river. A grassy landing area marked "no trespassing" serves as canoe access. Access from River Road, Mt. Bethel, Pennsylvania.

Map 22

203.2. Upstream end of Attins Island, with the main channel to the left.

202.9. Downstream end of Attins Island; upstream end of Thomas Island. Main channel continues on the left, but the passage between the islands is navigable. Thomas Island continues .2 mile downstream.

202.7. The site of Manunka Chunk, once an important rail junction, New Jersey side.

202.4. Upstream end of Dildine Island. The main channel is to the right and begins with a Class I rapid. The left channel is also passable, and opens into a maze of small islands, gravel bars, and winding passages. There are Class I rapids in some of these channels.

In the nineteenth and early twentieth century the Manunka Chunk House, a luxury hotel, occupied the island. The hotel burned to the ground in 1938. Today private cottages and boat landings dot Dildine Island.

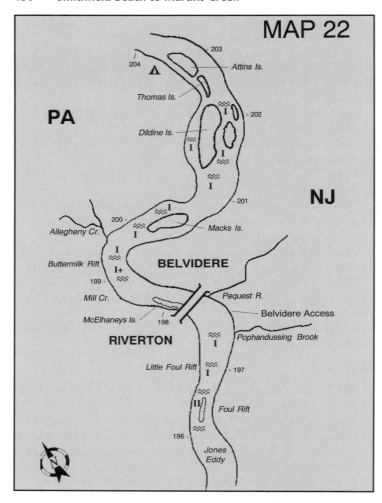

202.0. Lunch: King Cole Grove, a riverside ice cream stop and snack bar on U.S. Route 46 (New Jersey side), has a number of picnic tables on the riverbank.

201.4. Downstream end of Dildine Island.

A Class I rapid flows at the end of the channel on the Pennsylvania side.

201.0. River bends sharply right. This is the vicinity of the terminal moraine of the Wisconsin-era ice sheet, the last continental glacier in North America. Fifteen thousand years ago the area north of this point was buried under a mile of ice. The terminal moraine itself is an undulating mound of rocks extending from Staten Island, across New Jersey, through Pennsylvania, and into Ohio and the Midwest.

Hoffman-LaRoche Chemical Plant is on the New Jersey side. A water intake is marked by a buoy advising "stay away."

200.7. Pass under power lines.

200.6. Upstream end of Macks Island.

Long Rift, a Class I rapid, flows between the island and the Pennsylvania riverbank. The rift begins with a series of waves, then falls over a small rocky ledge 100 yards downstream from the head of the island. There is a second ledge near the downstream end of the island. The left channel is passable but shallow at low water level. Watch for the stony ledge where the left channel rejoins the main channel at the downstream end of the island.

200.0. A small unnamed creek enters, Pennsylvania side.

199.8. A small road approaches the river very closely on the Pennsylvania side. This is the site of Hartzell's Ferry, discontinued around 1900.

199.6. Allegheny Creek enters, Pennsylvania side, with a gravel bar constricting the river by nearly one-half.

Enter Buttermilk Rift, a Class I+ rapid. The main channel flows from the New Jersey side to the center of the river. Near the Pennsylvania side the channel is peppered with submerged and protruding boulders that require skillful maneuvering.

199.3. The second ledge of Buttermilk Rift. Watch for submerged rocks on the left.

199.1. The third and final ledge of Buttermilk Rift. The main channel is in the middle with standing waves to 2 feet. Submerged ledges extend from both banks.

198.8. Mill Creek enters, Pennsylvania side.

198.0. McElhaneys Island nestles near the Pennsylvania side. The narrow channel right (Pennsylvania side) of the island is not passable when the river level is low.

197.8. Pass under Riverton-Belvidere Bridge. The abutments and piers were constructed in 1836 to support a wooden bridge. The present four-span steel structure was built in 1904 after the old bridge was washed down in the Pumpkin Flood of 1903. It was in this vicinity that the rushing water of the Delaware tore pumpkins from their vines, littering the riverbanks downstream and giving the 1903 flood its name.

The communities of Riverton, Pennsylvania, and Belvidere, New Jersey, county seat of Warren County, stand at opposite ends of the bridge.

Lunch: Riverton Hotel and Restaurant, at Riverton end of bridge.

The Pequest River enters, New Jersey side, immediately downstream from the bridge.

The Martins Creek Land Management Area and Tekening Hiking Trails, owned and maintained by Pennsylvania Power and Light Company, Pennsylvania side, begin here. Hikers are welcome.

197.7. Belvidere access area, New Jersey, maintained by the New Jersey Division of Fish, Game and Shellfisheries. There is a gravel boat ramp, limited parking, and privies. Access from Front Street in Belvidere.

197.4. Pophandussing Creek, New Jersey side.

The gigantic concrete cooling towers of the Metropolitan Edison power plant loom ahead.

197.3. Enter Little Foul Rift, a Class I rapid. Shallows on the left and rock ledges on the right may be hazardous at low water. Main channel is through the center.

196.7. Enter Foul Rift, beginning as Class I but building quickly to a Class II rapid. The river drops 22 feet in the next .5 mile. Foul Rift begins with a cluster of angular boulders in the center of the river. There are passages left and right of center, but here, too, submerged and protruding rocks are a hazard.

Foul Rift, among the most severe rapids on the Delaware, should be avoided by beginners. There is no developed portage around the rapid, but at moderate water level canoeists can beach on the rocks along the New Jersey side and carry their canoes along the bars and ledges to calmer water.

196.6. Upstream end of Foul Rift Island, an exposed rock ledge parallel to the Pennsylvania riverbank. The narrow channel to the right of the island is passable with few obstructions and is the safest route. The main channel left of the island is peppered with boulders and ledges. Class II rapids.

196.5. Downstream end of Foul Rift Island. Exposed ledges extend from the New Jersey riverbank. The current flows from left to right. Rapids become more severe, with many submerged and protruding rocks. The safest passage remains near the Pennsylvania side.

196.3. The final ledge of Foul Rift, extending entirely across the river with a sudden drop of about 3 feet. At low water parts of the ledge are exposed, with a gap and high standing waves in the center. The channel near the Pennsylvania riverbank is also passable. This ledge was a severe hazard to timber rafts.

196.1. Numerous rock ledges and islands extend from the New Jersey riverbank for the next .2 mile. Clearest channel is along the Pennsylvania side.

Map 23

196.0. Enter Jones Eddy. Timber raftsmen pulled up here to collect their composure and equipment after running Foul Rift. Modern canoeists can do likewise.

195.8. Pass under power lines marked by red balls.

195.5. The coal-fired Metropolitan Edison Power Plant is on the Pennsylvania riverbank. The twin giant cooling towers are landmarks for miles around.

There are two water intakes for the power plant at the Pennsylvania riverbank, marked by signs: "DANGER—do not approach within 200 feet." Sound advice indeed.

194.9. Upstream end of Capush Island. The channel along the Pennsylvania side is impassable at low water.

Capush Rift, starting as Class I but building quickly to a Class I+ rapid, begins in the main channel left of the island. There is a broad gravel bar in the center of the channel. Just below this bar the river falls over a rock ledge; protruding and submerged rocks may be a hazard at low water. The best channel is in the middle with standing waves to 2 feet.

194.4. Capush Rift continues, falling over another ledge with shallows on the right. Best passage is in the left center of the river. Gravel bars on the right may be exposed at low water level.

194.3. Pass under bridge carrying railroad siding to Martins Creek power station.

Capush Rift ends under the bridge with standing waves to 2 feet in the middle and left of river.

194.2. Martins Creek access area, Pennsylvania, owned and maintained by the Pennsylvania Power and Light Company. There is a sandy boat ramp, parking, trash disposal, picnic tables, and privies. A gate to the area is locked from 9:00 P.M. to 7:00 A.M. Camping and overnight parking are not permitted.

Features

Delaware Water Gap National Recreation Area

The Delaware Water Gap National Recreation Area (DWGNRA) was planned originally as a complement to the Tocks Island Lake. It was expected that more than 10 million people a year would visit the park, primarily for lake-oriented recreation. The Tocks Island Dam was never built and, evidently, never will be. Beginning in 1966 the federal government acquired most of the land for the would-be lake bottom as well as additional lands along the river for recreational use. Seventy thousand acres are included in the recreation area, which is joined to Worthington and Stokes State Forests and High Point State Park. Almost all of the northwestern edge of New Jersey will be publicly owned for recreational use. With the demise of the dam and with the realization that local roads and services could not meet the demands of 10 million visitors a year, the National Park Service developed more modest plans for the administration and use of the recreation area. Low intensity recreation, such as hiking, nature study, hunting, fishing, and, of course, canoeing, is now regarded as the best use of the recreation area. Today, about four million people visit DWGNRA every year.

The population within the area encompassed by DWGNRA, especially the New Jersey portions, was never very great. Pahaquarry Township, which covers about 50 square miles, could claim only seven residents in 1996. When lands were acquired by the government for the lake and park, many of the residents had to leave, some of them against their will. Throughout the recreation area, especially along the Old Mine Road in New Jersey, the foundations of many abandoned and razed homes can be seen in the forest. The fertile lands along the river have always been excellent for a variety of crops, and considerable acreage within the park is used for farming under a permit system. Extensive cornfields can be seen from the river and along many of the roads within the park.

Cultural History. The National Park Service has a number of programs and exhibits devoted to interpreting the human history of the area. At the Slateford Farm, about one-half mile off Pennsylvania Route 611 (approximately Mile 209.5 on the river), an 1800s farmhouse has been reconstructed. Costumed interpreters conduct tours of the house and demonstrate nineteenth-century farming techniques. An abandoned slate quarry in the vicinity and may be visited on a guided nature walk that begins near the farm.

Millbrook Village, a partially reconstructed community of the nineteenth century, is found two miles north of the Depew access area on the Old Mine Road. The little village includes a blacksmith shop, general store, gristmill, church, school, and several historic homes. Reconstructed and used as they were 125 years ago, these buildings provide unusual insight into an American way of life long vanished. Millbrook had about 75 residents in the mid-1800s, but the little crossroads community dwindled as commerce concentrated in the cities. Until the park service acquired the lands in the 1970s, Millbrook remained a backwater of American history.

The historic Old Mine Road and Indian artifacts found within the DWGNRA are discussed in more detail in the features section of the preceding chapter.

An Environment for Art. The Delaware Water Gap has always been a favorite of artists, a tradition carried on in several programs sponsored by the National Park Service.

The entire community of Peters Valley, 2½ miles north of Walpack Center, is a living art studio. Woodwork, pottery, textiles, and metal sculpture are taught and practiced in what were once homes and barns. The studios themselves are closed to the public, but an information center and craft store are available to visitors. The Peters Valley crafts fair is held the last weekend of every July. Exhibits, demonstrations, and sales are clustered in a hayfield just up the hill from Peters Valley. This event attracts a great number of visitors every year. A visit to the crafts fair is a good way to begin or end a canoe trip.

Environmental Education. There are two centers for formal environmental education within the DWGNRA. These may be found at Walpack Center in New Jersey and at the Pocono Environmental Education Center (PEEC) four miles south of Dingmans Ferry on U.S. Route 209 in Pennsylvania (about Mile 234 on the river). PEEC was originally a honeymoon resort, but it is now used for classes and seminars in environmental studies. PEEC is available to groups, such as schools, church groups, scouts, clubs, and the like, for weekend or week-long in-residence educational programs. For more information, contact PEEC, RR 2, Box 1010, Dingmans Ferry, Pennsylvania 18328, 717-828-2319.

Interpretive nature walks are guided by park service experts at Dingmans Falls and other points of interest throughout the park. At Point of Gap, on the Pennsylvania riverbank at River Mile 211, an exhibit illustrates the geology of the water gap.

Information about current activities within the DWGNRA can be found at most of the National Park Service facilities. The Kittatinny Point information station, located at the Kittatinny Point access area (River Mile 211.7, New Jersey side), is easily accessible from the river and from I-80. Park service personnel are on hand to assist visitors—including canoeists—in enjoying the recreation area.

Delaware Water Gap

The Delaware Water Gap is the single most famous and spectacular natural feature along the Delaware River. Here the river has cut through the hard solid rock of the Kittatinny Ridge to form a cleft 1,300 feet deep, 1,500 yards across at the top and 300 yards across at the bottom. Kittatinny Mountain is a ridge of the Ridge and Valley geophysical province: a single, folded mountain extending from New York state, where it is known as the Shawangunk, through New Jersey, into Pennsylvania (where the ridge is known as Blue Mountain), and south into Maryland and Virginia (Shenandoah Mountain). Numerous other rivers cut through the ridge, including the Lehigh, Susquehanna, and Potomac.

The geologic formations of the water gap are well known. Hundreds of millions of years ago, during the Silurian period, the continents of Europe and North America were not separated. Great rivers flowed westward from ancient high mountains in Europe. Pebbles and sand were eroded from the mountains, carried off by rivers, and deposited over what is now eastern North America. As the mountains were eroded further and the sea level rose, the sediment became finer and finer until only sand, silt, and the debris of marine animals were deposited. These layers of sediment, thousands of feet thick, were compressed and solidified into rock. As the continents separated, intense pressure caused the layers of rock to heave and fold, creating new mountains.

29. The Delaware Water Gap as seen from the river. The river here has gouged a 1,300-foot-deep cleft in the Kittatinny Ridge. Photo by the author.

The remnants of these mountains exist today as the Ridge and Valley Province, including the Kittatinny Ridge. The layers of rock can be seen clearly at the Delaware Water Gap. The rocks tilt generally to the northwest, with the oldest rocks on the bottom.

Moving downstream through the water gap, the canoeist first encounters the red and greenish sandstones of the High Falls Formation (known in Pennsylvania as the Bloomsburg Formation). Indeed the river parallels the strike of this layer of rock for several miles above the water gap. In the middle of the gap the sandstone grades into a pebbly, gray-white conglomerate called the Shawangunk Formation. These are the sediments that rivers carried off from ancient European mountains to form the southeastern front of the Kittatinny Ridge. The layering of this rock can be seen clearly above landslides on both the Pennsylvania and New Jersey sides. A close inspection reveals intricate crossbedding caused by minor currents in the ancient rivers. Here and there in the Shawangunk Formation geologists have found very thin layers of shale that were formed by the deposition of silt and mud

in eddies of the ancient rivers. Fossils of extinct lobsterlike crea-
tures called eurypterids have been discovered in these black
deposits.

How the water gap itself was created is not certain. The Delaware River is deflected by the Kittatinny Ridge at Port Jervis and
runs parallel to the ridge until the river breaks through it at the
gap. It is likely that the river once flowed on a plane much higher
than at present, above the present-day Kittatinny Ridge. As
the river eroded overlying layers of rock, it maintained its
approximate course by cutting through a weak point in the
Shawangunk conglomerate formation. Over eons this weak point
was eroded deeper and deeper and eventually became the Delaware Water Gap. Glaciers in recent geologic history rounded and
shaped the gap into its present form. The water gap is still being
eroded, as evidenced by the great landslides on both sides.

The water gap was an early mecca for vacationers. In 1833 a
small hotel called Kittatinny House opened under the Pennsylvania cliffs at the water gap. In later decades of the nineteenth
century the water gap became even more popular with tourists
and artists. By 1877 the Kittatinny House was five stories high
and had hundreds of rooms. Several other Victorian-style hotels,
including the great Water Gap House, were built on the Pennsylvania banks. The hotels, however, eventually suffered by their
own intense rivalry and by improved transportation, which made
other tourist havens more accessible. One by one the grand old
hotels disappeared, until the Kittatinny House itself burned to
the ground in 1931. Today only its foundation remains.

The Appalachian Trail

White rectangles, precisely $2^{1}/_{2}$ inches wide by 6 inches tall, are
painted at intervals along the walkway on the I-80 bridge at the
Delaware Water Gap. From the Pennsylvania end of the bridge,
these blazes lead into the woods and may be followed all the way
to Springer Mountain, Georgia. From the New Jersey end of the
bridge the marks follow along Dunnfield Creek, past Sunfish Pond
atop Kittatinny Ridge, and eventually lead to Mt. Katahdin in
Maine. The white blazes identify the Appalachian Trail, a footpath that extends 2,015 miles along the ridge tops of the Appalachian Mountains.

The Appalachian Trail is not, as some think, an old Indian trail.
The Indians for the most part stayed in the valleys. Rather, the

trail can be credited primarily to one man, Benton MacKaye, who conceived the trail at the turn of the century and had the vision and perseverance to make it a reality.

The first section of the Appalachian Trail was marked and cleared in 1923 near Bear Mountain, New York. In 1937 the Civilian Conservation Corps axed the last portions of the trail through the swamps of Maine. The corridor of the Appalachian Trail is now protected by federal law, and in New Jersey all of the trail is on public land.

Until 1970 only a handful of people had actually hiked the entire trail from Georgia to Maine. But with the increased popularity of outdoor recreation, the number of "end-to-enders" mushroomed. Now, hundreds of hikers every year can claim rightly the coveted "Georgia to Maine" patch for their backpacks. Most people who hike the entire Appalachian Trail start in Georgia in early spring, then work their way north with the season, to arrive in Maine in September or October, just as snow begins to fall. To keep to this timetable the long-distance hikers must cross the Delaware in June or July.

End-to-end hikers are easy to spot. Unlike many day hikers, they don't seem to be in a hurry, yet cover the ground fast. Their shirts are worn to glossy smoothness at the shoulder. Their backpacks are a study in economy. Their boots are well oiled and in excellent repair, better than new. Every end-to-ender has his own personal reason for being on the trail. A man of about 60 explained that one day his wife left him; the next day he started walking the trail. He had never hiked before and said he never would again. He reshouldered his pack, tapped the tobacco in his pipe, and vanished alone into the forest toward Maine.

At the Delaware Water Gap the Appalachian Trial is easily accessible to canoeists. In New Jersey the trail leads from the DWGNRA Information Center under I-80 and through a dark hemlock ravine along cascading Dunnfield Creek. In about 3.75 miles the trail reaches Sunfish Pond, a crystal-clear lake carved by the glacier at the top of Kittatinny Ridge. This particular segment of the Appalachian Trail is among the most popular, and there are almost always a considerable number of hikers. The traffic has worn and eroded the footway, and much of the trail to Sunfish Pond is rough walking as a result. Unfortunately, too, inconsiderate hikers leave their litter behind them, making the trail less pleasant for others. National Park and State Park personnel, along with volunteers, police the area well, and there are frequent arrests for illegal camping and littering. A roundtrip hike to Sunfish Pond on the Appalachian Trail takes about five hours.

In Pennsylvania the Appalachian Trail leads steeply to the summit of Mt. Minsi (elevation 1,463 feet). This trail is somewhat less popular but affords outstanding overlooks of the Delaware Water Gap. It is about two miles—a roundtrip of three hours—to the summit.

An interesting, fairly easy side trail leads off the Appalachian Trail in New Jersey to the summit of Mt. Tammany (elevation 1,527 feet). This trail, marked by blue blazes, arrives at the summit after 2.5 miles for a panoramic view of the water gap and the river to the south. Hikers may return on the trail blazed with red dots to the rest area along I-80, a short distance east of the Kittatinny Information Center.

Martins Creek
to Upper Black Eddy

Mile 194.2 to 167.7 (26.5 miles)

Considerable perseverance is required to canoe the entire length of this section in one day; even the hardiest paddlers will be bone-tired when finished. This section is relatively little used by canoeists, although it is heavily used by recreational power boaters.

The river continues to flow through the Ridge and Valley geophysical province, and cuts through several small water gaps. Bedrock is exposed in many places, and ledges create numerous moderate rapids. Between rapids the pools are moderately deep, up to 35 feet below Raubsville. Just below Riegelsville the river leaves the Ridge and Valley and enters the Piedmont geophysical province, a broad band of rolling hills extending between New Jersey and northern Georgia. Between Riegelsville and Upper Black Eddy are found the 500-foot-high red sandstone Palisades of the Delaware. The Lehigh River, one of the Delaware's major tributaries, enters the river at the Forks of the Delaware at Easton, Pennsylvania.

Farmlands and forest continue to dominate the countryside along the river, with the exception of the twin cities of Phillipsburg, New Jersey, and Easton, Pennsylvania. In some areas, the river seems far from civilization and has a wilderness aspect; in other areas, cottages with private boat docks dot the riverbanks. U.S. Route 611 parallels the river on the Pennsylvania side between Martins Creek and Riegelsville. Below Riegelsville, Pennsylvania, Route 32 runs nearby.

The Delaware Canal, the last operating towpath canal in America, parallels the river on the Pennsylvania side below Easton. If there is sufficient water in the canal, canoeists can make use of the canal for circle trips. After travelling downstream on the river, canoeists can portage to the canal and return to the starting point upstream.

There are six public access points in this section:

Martins Creek, Pennsylvania, Mile 194.2
Sandts Eddy, Pennsylvania, Mile 189.9
Phillipsburg, New Jersey, Mile 184.0
Easton, Pennsylvania, Mile 183.7
Riegelsville, Pennsylvania, Mile 174.0
Upper Black Eddy, Pennsylvania, Mile 176.7.

Campsites can be found only at the very end of this section. The lands adjacent to the river and the river islands are, for the most part, privately owned.

River Guide

Map 23

194.2. Martins Creek access area, Pennsylvania, owned and maintained by the Pennsylvania Power and Light Company. There is a sandy boat ramp, parking, trash disposal, picnic tables, and privies. A gate to the area is locked from 9:00 P.M. to 7:00 A.M. Camping and overnight parking are not permitted.

Oughoughton Creek enters, Pennsylvania side.

The final waves of Capush Rift, now a Class I rapids, continue .1 mile.

193.4. A Class I rapid in a river "narrows." No major obstructions.

192.2. Buckhorn Creek enters, New Jersey side. River turns sharply right.

191.7. Water intakes for the Merrill Creek Reservoir, New Jersey side, constructed in 1988 to draw water for electric utilities. Buoys and signs advise "DANGER—submerged intake." Stay to the Pennsylvania side!

191.6. Keifer Island begins in the middle of the river. Smalleys Rift, a Class I rapid, begins in the left channel at the upstream end of the island. Standing waves to 1½ feet.

191.3. Keifer Island ends. Right channel turns sharply left to rejoin mainstream in a gravelly riffle. Smalleys Rift, a Class I rapid, continues in the left channel and mainstream, with a few boulders in right center.

191.2. Extensive gravel mining operations, New Jersey side.

190.7. Pass under railroad bridge.

Martins Creek enters, Pennsylvania side, immediately downstream from the bridge. Smokestacks of Martins Creek Cement

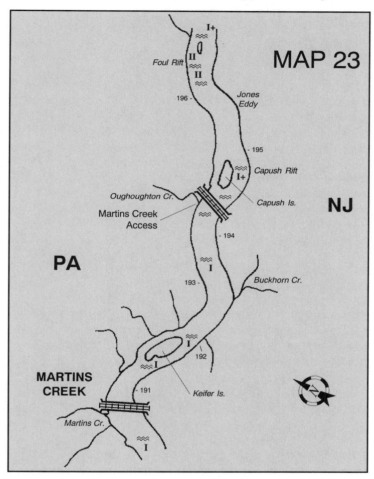

Plant are visible on the Pennsylvania side. Community of Martins Creek Station on New Jersey side.

Map 24

190.4. Martins Rift, a Class I rapid, with current moving slightly from right to left, in a constriction of the river. Gravel bars on New Jersey side.

189.9. A moderate riffle, then river slows into Sandts Eddy for next 2 miles. This area is very popular with motorboaters and Jet Skiers; canoeists should stay near either shore.

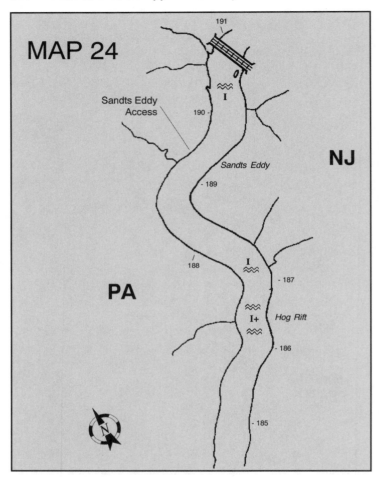

MAP 24

Sandts Eddy
Access

Sandts Eddy

NJ

PA

Hog Rift

189.3. Sandts Eddy access area, Pennsylvania, operated by the Pennsylvania Fish Commission. A boat ramp to the river, ample parking, trash disposal, and privies. Access from U.S. Route 611. All boats launched or landed here must bear a valid Pennsylvania boat registration.

189.2. Mud Run enters, Pennsylvania side.

187.5. Class I rapids near the Pennsylvania side, a series of ledges with few obstructions.

187.2. Another moderate riffle. River bends sharply to the right.

186.5. Frost Hollow Park, Pennsylvania, maintained by the

30. At Hog Rift, a Class I+ rapids just north of Easton, the Delaware passes through a mini water gap. Photo by the author.

North Hampton County Division of Parks and Recreation. A scenic overlook on Route 611 there is no good river access.

Enter Hog Rift. The rift is so named because at one time a great number of hogs, fatally poisoned from eating distillery slop, were thrown into the river near here and their carcasses came to lodge along the riverbanks. An 1860 map identifies the rapids as "Wygaat Falls."

Class I+ rapids begin at a diagonal ledge extending from the New Jersey riverbank. A parallel ledge that reaches nearly across the river follows. Clear passage is possible around either end of the second ledge; openings in the ledge itself may be found by aiming for a conspicuous downstream "V." Big rocks protrude from the river.

One hundred yards downstream the river constricts at the last plunge of Hog Rift; clear passage with high standing waves near the Pennsylvania side. The river is peppered with boulders and ledges, requiring quick maneuvers.

186.2. River passes between Chestnut Hill (Pennsylvania) and Marble Mountain (New Jersey) a mini water gap. There are high limestone bluffs on both sides.

185.7. A large gravel bar on the New Jersey side extends to the middle of the river. Passage to the right is clear.

185.3. The City of Easton water treatment plant stands on the bluff, Pennsylvania side, above a concrete bulkhead. Water from the Delaware River is treated for consumption by city residents. Pass under power lines.

Map 25

185.0. Eddyside Park river swimming area, maintained by the City of Easton. There is also a swimming pool open to the public for a fee. There is no good canoe access.

184.3. Getters Island begins. Its slender upstream tip nearly touches the Pennsylvania riverbank. Getters Island is named for Charles Getter, who was publicly hanged at the site in 1833 for the murder of his wife. In 1860, the steamboat *Alfred Thomas* exploded while beached at Getters Island, killing at least 10 passengers.

The channel to the right of Getters Island is passable, ending at a low dam at the downstream end of the island. A chute in the center of the dam makes an exciting quick drop into high standing waves. At moderately high water, the dam is submerged and should not be attempted, owing to a potentially dangerous hydraulic.

There is a Class I rapid in the main channel to the left of Getters Island. The best route is straight down the middle. Watch for boulders.

184.1. Getters Island ends. Bushkill Creek enters, Pennsylvania side. This is the third "Bushkill Creek" to enter the Delaware River.

184.0. Pass beneath the Easton-Phillipsburg Toll Bridge. This single steel-truss span was constructed in 1938. There is a moderate riffle under the bridge.

Phillipsburg access area, New Jersey, maintained by the City of Phillipsburg, New Jersey, just downstream from the bridge. Includes parking, a boat ramp, trash disposal, and water.

The City of Easton, Pennsylvania, population 26,276 (1990), the largest community on the Delaware River above Trenton, is on the right. Phillipsburg, New Jersey, population 16,647 (1990), is on the left. There are plenty of restaurants and other services in both cities.

183.9. Pass under North Hampton Street Bridge. A wooden

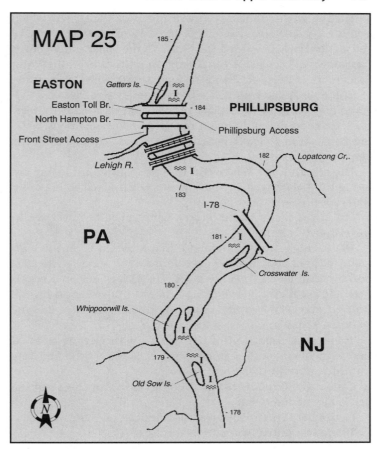

MAP 25   185

EASTON   Getters Is.

Easton Toll Br.   184   PHILLIPSBURG
North Hampton Br.
Front Street Access   Phillipsburg Access

Lehigh R.   182   Lopatcong Cr,.

183
I-78

PA   181

Crosswater Is.
180

Whippoorwill Is.

NJ
179

Old Sow Is.

N   178

structure upon stone piers was built at this site in 1806, one of the first bridges to span the Delaware. The present bridge, with new abutments, was completed in 1895. Its cantilever-truss design is unique on the Delaware.

183.8. Lunch: There is a dirt landing area on the New Jersey side, with wooden stairs leading up the bluff to Union Square cafe/general store and Eddie's Drive-in.

183.7. Easton Front Street Park access area, Pennsylvania, maintained by the City of Easton. There is a paved boat ramp, parking, trash disposal, and pay phone. Access from U.S. Route 611 in Easton, just upstream from the confluence of the Lehigh River.

The Lehigh River enters, Pennsylvania side. The Lehigh, which drains a considerable area of northeast Pennsylvania, is one of the major tributaries of the Delaware. To the Lenape, the Lehigh was known as Lechauwiechink; early colonists called it the "West Branch of the Delaware," and the main stem of the Delaware the "East Branch." The confluence of the Lehigh and Delaware Rivers is the "Forks of the Delaware," a commercial and strategic prize for centuries and a main objective of the infamous Walking Purchase of 1737, in which the area was acquired from the Lenape.

The Lehigh River falls over a 12-foot spillway just before entering the Delaware. This spillway was constructed to impound water for the Delaware Canal.

This is the site of Martin's Ferry, which plied the Delaware in the eighteenth century.

183.6. Hugh Moore Park and Canal Museum is on the bluff (Pennsylvania side) just downstream from the Forks. There are a dozen picnic tables with fire grills. The Delaware Canal begins here and parallels the river for 60 miles to tidewater at Bristol, Pennsylvania. (The features section of this chapter describes the Delaware Canal in more detail.)

There is an elaborate fish passageway, with viewing areas, at the southern end of the Lehigh spillway, allowing fish to migrate into and out of the Lehigh.

Canoes can be easily beached, so canoeists can check out the fish ladder and museum.

Pass under Lehigh Valley Railroad Bridge.

183.5. Pass under twin railroad bridges.

183.3. Class I rapids, continuing .2 mile; very shallow on the left, watch for boulders on the right.

182.4. City of Easton wastewater treatment plant is on the bluff, Pennsylvania side. The outfall from the plant can be seen as a gray frothy discharge, which the river quickly assimilates. At one time, most communities along the Delaware discharged their untreated wastewater directly into the river; now, all discharges are treated to at least "secondary" (biological treatment) standards and subject to compliance with a discharge permit.

182.1. Rock garden and ledges on the right; can be fun maneuvering among the boulders.

182.0. Pass under power lines.

181.9. Lopatcong Creek enters, New Jersey side.

River bends sharply right.

181.2. The massive concrete and steel bridge carrying Interstate Route 78 towers above the river. Constructed in 1989, this is the newest bridge across the Delaware.

181.0. Crosswater Island, a gravel bar with trees on the downstream end. At moderately low water level, the island touches the Pennsylvania riverbank.

There is a short Class I rapid in the channel to the left (New Jersey side) of the island.

A small stream enters, New Jersey side, at the center of the island, creating a gravel bar that extends 15 yards into the river.

179.8. Whippoorwill Islands. There is a strong Class I rapid along the New Jersey side—a sharp drop and choppy waves. The channel to the right of Whippoorwill Island (Pennsylvania side) is impassable at low water.

179.4. River bends sharply left downstream of Whippoorwill Island. There are numerous boat docks on the New Jersey riverbank for the next .4 mile.

178.9. Old Sow Island, with a broad gravel bar at its upstream end.

A strong Class I rapid in the left channel flows around two small gravel bars. Passage is clear in the channel closest to Old Sow Island.

A rock ledge 100 yards downstream from the head of Old Sow Island in the right channel, extending from the Pennsylvania side, creates large standing waves. Class I rapids continue to the end of the island.

Lunch: Raubsville Tavern has a riverside landing for boaters at the downstream end of Old Sow Island, Pennsylvania side.

Map 26

178.5. A small unnamed creek enters through a culvert and over a falls, New Jersey side.

178.4. Community of Raubsville, Pennsylvania side. This is the site of Raub's Ferry, which plied the Delaware in the early nineteenth century.

177.6. A whitewashed stone building stands at the river's edge, Pennsylvania side. This was once a mini hydroelectric plant, diverting water from the Delaware Canal. Some of the mechanism can be viewed from a walkway around the structure.

A dirt landing area and wooden steps just downstream from

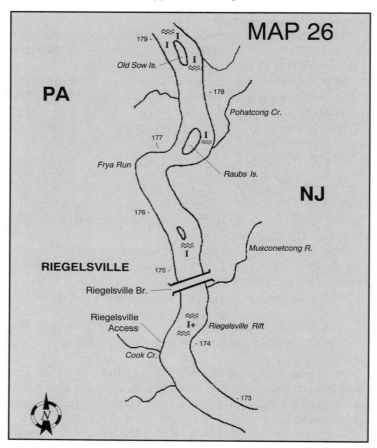

the old power plant lead to Locks 22–23 of the Delaware Canal. There are picnic tables, fire grills, trash disposal, privies, and a water pump. This is a good place to stop for a rest or picnic lunch.

177.5. Raubs Island, also known as Groundhog Island. In moderately low water the right (Pennsylvania side) channel is dry. Pass under power lines.

177.4. Class I rapids.

177.3. Pohatcong Creek enters, New Jersey side, with large gravel bars extending to the middle of the channel.

The river here is pressed into a narrow channel, developing treacherous eddies, boils, and whirlpools.

177.2. Raubs Island ends.

River turns sharply right.

Sharp rocky ledges protrude from water and extend from New Jersey side. To old-time river raftsmen, who came downriver during spring floods, this formation was known as "Rocky Falls."

176.7. Frya Run Park, on U.S. Route 611, Pennsylvania side, operated by the North Hampton County Park Board. There is limited parking, and a rough trail access to the river. There is no good place to launch a boat. A reconstructed historic stone-arch bridge highlights the park.

Frya Run enters, Pennsylvania side. The Pennsylvania Canal crosses Frya Run in a wooden aqueduct clearly visible from the river.

176.5. Angular ledges protrude from water for next .5 mile. Be alert for submerged rocks. Fun to maneuver among the rocks.

River bends sharply left. There is a moderate current.

176.0. Limestone cliffs, New Jersey side.

175.5. A large gravel bar in the middle of the river.

175.4. A Class I rapid with no obstructions.

174.8. Pass under the Riegelsville Bridge. A wooden bridge was built here in 1835. The present twin-cable suspension bridge, one of the most picturesque spans across the Delaware, was completed in 1904.

The communities of Riegelsville, Pennsylvania, and Riegelsville, New Jersey, stand at opposite ends of the bridge.

Lunch: Riegelsville Hotel and cafe, other casual restaurants at Pennsylvania end of Riegelsville bridge.

174.7. Musconetcong River enters, New Jersey side, under an abandoned building of the Riegel Paper Company.

174.4. Riegelsville Rift, a Class I+ rapids. A rocky ledge about three feet high extends diagonally from the New Jersey side. At moderate level skilled canoeists can identify and sneak through gaps in the ledge near the New Jersey side. Passage is clear, with standing waves, near the Pennsylvania side.

174.0. Riegelsville access area, Pennsylvania. Maintained by the Pennsylvania Fish and Boat Commission. There is a steep dirt ramp to the river, ample parking, trash disposal, and privies. All boats must bear a valid Pennsylvania boat registration.

173.9. Cook Creek (also known as Durham Creek) enters, Pennsylvania side, with a gravel bar extending one-third of the way across the river. Lock 21 and the Durham Aqueduct of the

31. Riegelsville suspension bridge, constructed in 1904. Photo by the author.

Delaware Canal can be seen a short distance up Cook Creek. There are historic markers and a few picnic tables. Rough access from the river.

This was the site of Durham furnace, which produced iron from 1698 until 1908. Robert Durham, who operated the furnace here, developed the famous Durham boats that were used by George Washington in his crossing of the Delaware in 1776 and by tradesmen for many years along the river.

A crossing called Parsley Ferry ran here in the nineteenth century.

The river is pooled for the next 1.6 miles.

Map 27

172.3. Lynn Island. The main channel is on the left (New Jersey) side of the island, with a Class I rapid. Rock ledges on the New Jersey side are a possible hazard. A gravel bar extending from the New Jersey riverbank at the downstream end of Lynn Island constricts the river into another Class I rapid.

The channel to the right (Pennsylvania side) of Lynn Island is narrow but passable, and is more interesting than the main

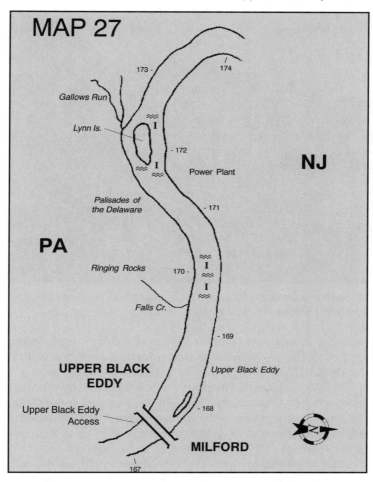

MAP 27

173 -   174

Gallows Run

Lynn Is.   I   - 172

I   Power Plant   NJ

Palisades of
the Delaware   - 171

PA

Ringing Rocks   170 -   I
                              I

Falls Cr.

- 169

UPPER BLACK   Upper Black Eddy
EDDY

Upper Black Eddy   - 168
Access

MILFORD

167

channel. There is a good Class I rapids about halfway down the right channel, requiring maneuvering around boulders.

172.2. Gallows Run enters, Pennsylvania side.

171.9. Lynn Island ends. A vegetated gravel island lies in the center of the Pennsylvania channel, with a Class I rapids on either side.

Lock 20 on the Delaware Canal, with a few picnic tables nearby, is on the Pennsylvania riverbank.

The Palisades of the Delaware, also known as the "Narrows of Nockamixen," rise 500 feet from the river on the Pennsylvania

32. The Palisades of the Delaware. Red sandstone cliffs tower above the river below Riegelsville. Photo by the author.

side. The palisades are composed of red sandstone and shale and are part of the Stockton Formation, which extends into central Connecticut.

171.7. The Gilbert Generating Station, operated by New Jersey Power and Light Company, is on the New Jersey riverbank. Cooling water is discharged from a concrete outfall extending from the river's edge. Several high-tension lines cross the river in the vicinity.

171.0. Canoeists with vivid imaginations might see the profile of a human head in the rock formations atop the palisades.

170.2. A series of rock ledges extend across the river. Passage through the ledges may be obstructed, but is sure near the Pennsylvania side.

170.0. Camping. Bucks County River Country (Point Pleasant Canoes), Pennsylvania side, has a riverside campground with tent sites, picnic tables, and sanitary facilities.

169.0. Falls Creek enters, Pennsylvania side.

Enter Upper Black Eddy, slow water for the next mile.

167.7. Pass under Milford–Upper Black Eddy Bridge. The original wooden bridge was built in 1842; the present three-span steel truss was completed in 1933. A ferry known as London Ferry ran here before the bridge was constructed.

The communities of Upper Black Eddy, Pennsylvania, and Milford, New Jersey, stand at opposite ends of the bridge. The village of Milford was once called Sunburn.

Lunch: cafe and general store in Upper Black Eddy, many casual restaurants in Milford.

Upper Black Eddy access area, Pennsylvania, maintained by the Pennsylvania Fish Commission, is located just downstream from the Milford–Upper Black Eddy bridge. There is ample parking, a boat ramp, privies, and trash disposal. All boats must bear a valid Pennsylvania boat registration. Access from Pennsylvania Route 32.

Features

Easton, Pennsylvania/Phillipsburg, New Jersey

Except for Trenton, at the end of the canoeable Delaware River, Easton, Pennsylvania (population 26,276), is the largest community to be encountered on the banks of the river. Located at the strategic Forks of the Delaware, Easton was founded in 1752 by Thomas Penn, a son of William Penn. The site was acquired in the infamous Walking Purchase in 1737. Easton grew quickly as one of America's first industrial centers in the early nineteenth century. It was a meeting place of three canals—the Lehigh Canal, which extended into the mountain coal fields; the Morris Canal, which crossed New Jersey to the Hudson River; and the Delaware Canal, which parallels the river to tidewater at Bristol. Five major railroads also came to Easton, making the city a hub of regional commerce.

The people of Easton have recently made an effort to highlight the heritage of their city. Easton is part of the National Main Street Program, a special demonstration project of the National Trust for Historic Preservation. A self-guided walking tour takes visitors past more than 30 buildings remarkable for their historic interest or architecture, ranging from a tavern built in 1754 to Art Deco commercial buildings. In Center Square, only two blocks from the river, an outdoor farmers' market operates every Tuesday, Thursday, and Saturday.

Easton offers all the services to be expected in a city of its size. There are numerous restaurants from fast food to fancy fare, shopping centers, movie theaters, several motels, and cultural activities. For specific information contact the Two Rivers Area Commerce Council, 157 South Fourth Street, Easton, Pennsylvania 18042, 215-253-4211.

Phillipsburg, New Jersey, population 16,647, stands immediately across the river from Easton. The Phillipsburg area was sparsely settled until 1832 when the Morris Canal was opened, linking the Delaware River with the Hudson River at Newark. Phillipsburg became a seaport 60 miles from tidewater, and it grew further with the arrival of railroads in 1852. The canal is long gone, yet Phillipsburg remains an important regional center. There are numerous grocery stores, restaurants, a motel, and shops within walking distance from the river.

The Delaware Canal

The boom days of towpath canals were largely over by the turn of the century. The greater efficiency and speed of railroads made it impossible for the canals to compete. By 1930 most of the old canals were long abandoned and in ruins. But today there are many people living in the Pennsylvania communities along the Delaware River below Easton who readily recall the barges loaded with lumber and coal that once plied the Delaware Canal. The canal, which connected Easton and tidewater at Bristol, was operated commercially until 1931, outlasting all the other towpath canals in America.

Beginning with construction of the Erie Canal in 1825, the road to westward expansion was paved with water. Over the next several decades about 4,000 miles of towpath canals were constructed in eastern America, enabling the tentacles of commerce to penetrate the wilderness. Pennsylvania alone had 1,200 miles of canals, more than any other state. The Mainline Canal from Philadelphia to Pittsburgh, the Union Canal along the Schuylkill River, and the Delaware and Hudson Canal (which crosses into New York at Lackawaxen) were all part of this extensive system. In 1829 the Lehigh Canal was completed from the coal country of the Pocono Mountains to Easton. The Delaware Canal, completed in 1832, in turn connected Easton to the tidewater Delaware River at Bristol. Hardrock coal mined in the mountains could be barged to market at Philadelphia in a few days. During the peak years in the mid-nineteenth century, over 3,000 boats travelled over the canal annually. Ultimately, about 33 million tons of coal and 6 million tons of other cargoes would be mule-barged to market.

Life on the canal was hard from the beginning. The canal was constructed mostly by Irish immigrants and local farmers on contract, who worked only with hand tools and occasionally with horses. Workdays were long, pay was low, and the labor strenuous. Each barge was a standard 87½ feet long, by 10½ feet wide and drew 5 feet of water when loaded. The barge was piloted by a crew of two, often husband and wife. A team of two mules, walking ahead on the towpath, pulled the barge along the canal. The crew would stop only to rest the mules or to exchange teams. The locktenders, who lived in company houses adjacent to the canal, were on call around the clock to pass traffic through the locks.

Soon after the canal was abandoned, it became used increasingly for recreation. Fishing, canoeing, and travelling on party barges became regular activities on the canal. In 1940 the Commonwealth of Pennsylvania established a park running the length of the canal.

Because it was commercially operated and maintained as late as 1931, the Delaware Canal remains in excellent condition along its 60-mile course. The canal is never more than a few hundred yards from the Delaware River, and in places it is separated from the river only by an earthen berm. Numerous points of interest along the canal are easily accessible from the Delaware River. The canal can be used to make a "circle" canoe trip, which involves paddling downstream on the river and then returning upstream by canal to the starting point. There is a slight current in the canal, but this can be countered easily in a canoe.

The best place to learn about the canal is the Hugh Moore State Park and Canal Museum at Easton. Access to the museum is easily made just downstream from the confluence of the Delaware and Lehigh Rivers. The museum contains several excellent exhibits, including a full-size mock-up of a barge cabin, a gallery of canal art, implements and tools used in canal operation, scale models of canal construction, and an old movie of mules pulling a barge through a lock. (The movie should not be missed.) There is a modest admission fee. The museum is at the canal's starting point, and the principal gate lock is just outside.

There are 23 lift locks along the canal, most of which are operational. The lift locks, which were used to raise and lower boats

33. Delaware Canal lock in Delaware Canal State Park, Pennsylvania. The canal once carried barge traffic from Easton to Bristol. Photo by the author.

between different water levels, consist of narrow stone channels with massive wooden gates at both ends. The water level in the channel could be raised or lowered to bring the barge in line with the adjacent canal section. Several of these locks may be visited easily from the river, including Durham Lock at Mile 173.8; Narrows Lock at Mile 171.9; Lewis Lock at Mile 160.5; Whites Double Lock at Mile 156.8 (just below Point Pleasant); Lumberville Lock at Mile 155.5 (slightly upstream from the Lumberville Foot Bridge); and Locks 9, 10, and 11 at Mile 148, which raise the canal level along Wells Falls at New Hope. The remaining locks, of course, may be found by canoeing or walking along the canal itself.

In numerous places the canal had to cross streams and rivers. For this purpose aqueducts were constructed to contain the canal as it bridged a stream below. Some of the aqueducts that may be seen include Durham Aqueduct, which is partially dismantled, at Mile 173.8; Gallows Run Aqueduct, by Lynn Island, at Mile 172.1; Tinicum Creek Aqueduct, one of the highest, at Mile 161.6; Tohicon Creek Aqueduct at Point Pleasant, Mile 157.0; Stony Run Aqueduct at Mile 144.0; and Brock Creek Aqueduct at Yardley, which may be seen by paddling a short distance up Brock Creek, Mile 138.0.

Mule-drawn barge rides are open to the public in New Hope every day between Memorial Day and Labor Day. Passenger barges are hauled up the canal 4 1/2 miles, then returned to New Hope. The rides makes for a different and relaxing side trip and gives passengers a taste of what life may have been like on the old Delaware Canal.

Ringing Rocks

Atop the Palisades of the Delaware near Upper Black Eddy is an exposure of angular boulders. No soil has developed in this four-acre clearing, nor has any vegetation taken root. The field of boulders has an artificial appearance, as if it were placed there on purpose by the working of hundreds of dump trucks. But the exposure is entirely natural, and when the rocks in this clearing are struck with a hammer, they ring like bells. This curiosity has been long known as Ringing Rocks, and a county park has been established here to protect the site.

When J. Wallace Hoff canoed the Delaware in 1892 he characterized Ringing Rocks as "a collection of metallic boulders that emit ringing and even musical combinations upon being struck." Indeed, with a few friends, simple melodies can be played by striking different rocks at the right time. As a rule, the larger boulders produce bass tones, while smaller ones are treble. The Ringing Rocks are composed of rather fine conglomerate stone. Though some have suggested that a metallic content is responsible for the resonance, it is more likely that interior stress caused by repeated freezing and thawing produces the bell-like tones.

Ringing Rocks can be reached from the river in two ways. The easiest one involves walking up Bridgeton Hill Road (which intersects Pennsylvania Route 32 .2 mile north of the Upper Black Eddy–Milford Bridge) .8 mile to Ringing Rocks Road, then turning right, and continuing .2 mile to the park entrance. A more adventurous route requires bushwhacking up Falls Creek, an intermittent stream that flows into the Delaware at Mile 169.0. (Caution: Another small stream meets the Delaware immediately upstream from the confluence of the Delaware and Falls Creek; Falls Creek, unlike its neighbor, intersects the Delaware Canal and Pennsylvania Route 32 a short distance from the river.) The stream tumbles over a series of sandstone and shale ledges through a deep hemlock ravine that ends upstream at a solid rock wall. A wide trail to the right of the wall leads to the Ringing Rocks.

Upper Black Eddy to Lambertville

Mile 167.7 to 148.6 (19.1 miles)

This section of the river passes through 19 miles of mixed forests and farmlands. The rolling hills are characteristic of the Piedmont geophysical province, and outcrops of sandstone and shale rock tower above the river in places. Generally, the river is very shallow, with long gentle pools separated by mild rapids. There are no severe rifts in this section, though rapids at the end of Prahls Island and at the Lumberville wing dams offer excitement. A 2½-mile-long maze of islands beginning at Mile 162.6 provides many narrow channels to be explored.

Pennsylvania Route 32 and the Delaware Canal run parallel and very close to the river on the Pennsylvania side. The historic villages of Upper Black Eddy, Erwinna, Point Pleasant, Lumberville, and New Hope are nestled along the riverbank. Several genteel inns dating from the early nineteenth century can be found along Route 32. Most of the old inns offer lodging and a style of hospitality that has long disappeared in most of the country.

New Jersey Route 29 closely follows the river on the other side. The Delaware and Raritan (D&R) Feeder Canal begins at Bulls Island, then parallels the river to Lambertville and beyond. The D&R Canal as well as the Delaware Canal in Pennsylvania can be used for circle canoe trips, which involve canoeing downstream on the river, then paddling upstream on the canal to the starting point. The communities of Milford, Frenchtown, Stockton, and Lambertville began as ferry points on the river and retain a distinct historical flavor.

Six public access areas make it easy to get on the river in this section:

Upper Black Eddy Access (Pennsylvania), Mile 167.7
Kingwood Access (New Jersey), Mile 163.4
Tinicum County Park (Pennsylvania), Mile 162.9

Byram Access (New Jersey), Mile 156.1
Bulls Island Recreation Area, Mile 155.2
Lambertville Access, Mile 148.6.

There are three camping areas, including Tinicum County Park and Bulls Island Recreation Area right on the riverbanks. Land along the river and river islands are otherwise privately owned, and trespassing is discouraged.

River Guide

Map 28

167.7. Upper Black Eddy access area, Pennsylvania, maintained by the Pennsylvania Fish Commission, is located just downstream from the Milford–Upper Black Eddy bridge. There is ample parking, a boat ramp, privies, and trash disposal. All boats must bear a valid Pennsylvania boat registration. Access from Pennsylvania Route 32.

The community of Upper Black Eddy is on the Pennsylvania riverbank. Upper Black Eddy was an important stop on the Delaware Canal and a popular stopping place for timber raftsmen in the eighteenth and nineteenth centuries. The old Upper Black Eddy Inn still stands between the river and canal, .8 mile upstream from the bridge. The community of Milford, New Jersey, is at the eastern end of the bridge.

167.2. Hakihokake Creek enters, New Jersey side. Gravel bars at the mouth of the stream extend about 20 yards into the river.

167.1. Pass under power lines.

167.0. A series of five small brushy gravel bars dot the middle of the river for the next half mile. The river is very shallow between the islands.

The smokestacks and water tower of the Riegel Paper Company's Milford plant can be seen on the New Jersey side. Riegel Paper is one of the major industries along the Delaware River, producing printing, packaging, and specialty papers. The water discharge from the plant flows from a pipe at the river's edge.

166.8. A small unnamed creek enters, New Jersey side, with gravelly shallows near the mouth of the stream.

166.6. A very mild riffle marks the end of Upper Black Eddy.

166.5. Camping. Dog Wood Haven Campground (R.D. 1, Box 615, Lodi Hill Road, Upper Black Eddy, Pennsylvania 18972, 215-982-5402). Accessible from the Upper Black Eddy access area,

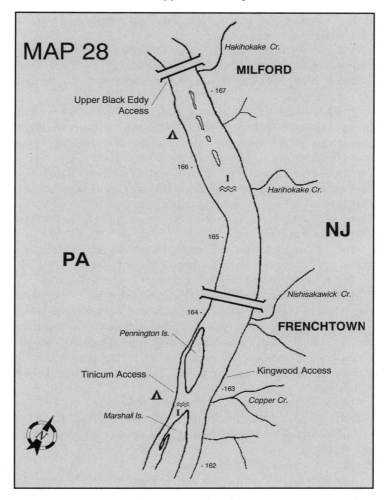

about one mile from the river. Dog Wood Haven is operated by Pennsylvania's Delaware Canal State Park. There are a limited number of sites available with picnic tables and charcoal grills.

166.0. Pass under power lines.

165.7. A Class I rapids begins with a submerged ledge extending diagonally from the New Jersey bank, then a second ledge straight across the river about 40 yards downstream. The best passage is on the left: look for gaps in the ledge with standing waves below.

Harihokake Creek enters, New Jersey side, with grassy gravel bars extending downstream.

165.4. River bends slightly right. Moderate riffle across river, with minor obstructions on the extreme left.

165.0. Rocky ledges along New Jersey side extend into the river for next .2 mile.

164.3. Pass under Uhlerstown-Frenchtown Bridge. A wooden bridge was first built here in 1843. The present six-span steel truss was erected in 1931 on the original abutments and piers. The town of Frenchtown, New Jersey, originally called Alexandria, is on the left. Uhlerstown, Pennsylvania, formerly known as Mexico, was a whistle-stop on the Delaware Canal. There are several interesting old buildings dating from the canal's heyday. There is a lovely historic covered bridge one mile from the river on Uhlerstown Road.

164.2. Nishisakawick Creek enters, New Jersey side, with a large gravel bar extending nearly to the middle of the river.

164.1. Little Nishisakawick Creek enters, New Jersey side.

163.8. Mile-long Pennington Island begins on the extreme right side of the river. The narrow channel between the island and the Pennsylvania riverbank is passable in a canoe at moderate water level, but not recommended. A footbridge crosses the channel about halfway through. The Presbyterian Church runs a camp on the island, and the present owners call the island "New Life Island."

163.4. Kingwood public access area, New Jersey, operated by the New Jersey Division of Fish, Game, and Wildlife. There is a concrete boat ramp, ample parking, privies. Access from New Jersey Route 29.

163.0. Pennington Island ends.

162.9. Tinicum County Park access area, Pennsylvania, maintained by the Bucks County Department of Parks and Recreation. There is a concrete boat ramp, parking, trash disposal, telephone, water, and sanitary facilities. Access from Pennsylvania Route 32.

Camping. Tinicum County Park, Pennsylvania, with picnic tables, fresh water, grills, and privies. Good tent sites, with easy access to the river.

The historic Irwin Stover House, open to the public, is located near the river in Tinicum County Park.

162.8. Copper Creek enters, New Jersey side.

Map 29

162.5. Beginning of Marshall Island, which extends nearly 2 miles downstream, in the middle of the river. Marshall was once known as Man-of-War Island because tall trees on the upstream end resembled the masts of a battleship. The tall trees, however, are gone. The island's present name is derived from the Marshall family, which included Edward Marshall, one of the runners participating in the infamous Walking Purchase of 1737 (see feature about Tom Quick).

Marshall Island begins a maze of 11 islands that extends 2$\frac{1}{2}$ miles along the Delaware. Exploring the little channels among the islands is an adventure in itself. Access to these channels is somewhat easier from the left side of Marshall Island.

Marshall Island, together with Treasure Island immediately downstream, is owned by the Philadelphia Council of the Boy Scouts of America. A scout camp started here in 1913 is today the oldest Boy Scout camp in the United States. No trespassing.

162.4. The Old Stover Mill, built in 1832 and one of the earliest turbine-wheel mills in the country, stands at the very edge of the river on the Pennsylvania riverbank. The mill is now maintained as a museum, library, and art gallery. The historic Isaac Stover House (1837), open to the public, stands across Route 32 from the mill.

A rocky ledge extends from the base of the mill to the tip of a large gravel bar in the center of the channel, making for a Class I rapid. At low water the ledge can be breached only at its center.

161.8. Pass under power lines.

161.7. A small creek enters under an aqueduct, Pennsylvania side.

161.5. Tinicum Creek enters, Pennsylvania side. A high aqueduct of the Delaware Canal crosses Tinicum Creek about 50 yards from the river. A large gravel bar extends into the river channel.

Pinkertons Island begins, left channel (New Jersey side).

161.4. Fishing Island and Resolution Island nestle near the Pennsylvania side.

161.3. Shyhawks Island begins, left channel (New Jersey side).

On clear days canoeists often see antique biplanes, gliders, ultralights, and other unusual aircraft flying over the Delaware. These originate from Van Sant Airport, a grass strip 2 miles from the river in Pennsylvania.

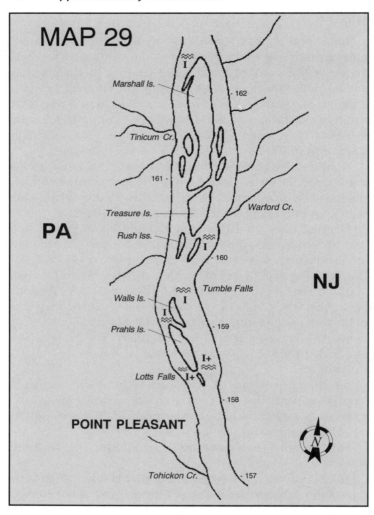

160.8. End Marshall Island; begin Treasure Island. The narrow channel separating the islands is spanned by a precarious wooden suspension bridge.

There are mild riffles in the channels both left and right around Treasure Island.

The boundary line between New Jersey and Pennsylvania passes down the narrow channel between Marshall Island (Pennsylvania) and Treasure Island (New Jersey).

34. Canoeists pass historic Stover Mill at Erwinna, Pennsylvania, now an art gallery and museum. Photo by the author.

160.7. Boy Scouts are ferried from the Pennsylvania riverbank to their camp on Treasure Island via canoes or a little ferry reminiscent of the scows used to cross the Delaware in the nineteenth century.

160.4. Warford Creek enters, New Jersey side. Mild riffle in left channel.

160.2. Treasure Island ends. There are moderate riffles near the island on both sides.

Rush Islands, extending .2 mile downstream, begin in left center and right center of the river, forming three channels: Pennsylvania, middle, and New Jersey. The state line here runs between the islands.

160.1. Class I rapids run in the New Jersey and middle channels. A rocky ledge extends to the middle of the channel from the New Jersey side.

The Devils Tea Table, a pedestal-shaped rock formation, can be seen high on the sandstone cliffs on the New Jersey side.

159.3. River bends widely left. A series of flat ledges known as Tumble Falls extends from the New Jersey side nearly across the river. At moderate water level it is possible to maneuver through various clefts between the ledges, although canoes can easily get stuck and stranded on the flat rocks. In slightly higher water, the ledges are submerged and present a Class I rapid. There is always clear passage near the Pennsylvania side.

The community on the New Jersey side was once known as Tumble.

Begin Walls Island in the middle of the river. There is a moderate riffle along the right (Pennsylvania) side. Go to the right (Pennsylvania side) of Walls Island to catch exciting Lotts Falls downstream.

159.1. A narrow channel between Walls Island and Prahls Island, diagonally left from Pennsylvania side. There is a Class I rapid with high standing waves in the channel. Canoeists must not take this inviting course if they wish to run the more challenging Lotts Falls downstream; instead, continue to hug the Pennsylvania side.

Three rocky ledges cross the left channel (New Jersey side) in the next .2 mile make a series of Class I rapids.

158.3. Right (Pennsylvania side) of Prahls Island: Lotts Falls, an exciting Class I+ rapids (II– at moderately high water). Boulders and ledges protrude from the water and lurk just below the surface, requiring quick maneuvers to avoid upset. At moderately high water, a ledge on the left at the end of the rapids is a problem.

158.2. End Prahls Island.

Left channel: Begin Class I rapid extending .1 mile to end of gravel bar. Standing waves to 2 feet can be found in the right center of the channel.

157.2. Three piers of the old Point Pleasant Bridge stand in the river. The bridge was washed out in the 1955 hurricane.

Point Pleasant was once an important stop on the Delaware Canal. Today there are numerous antique shops and galleries here.

Bucks County River Country (Point Pleasant Canoe and Tube) main base is on the Pennsylvania side at the bridge abutment. Private canoes may be launched for a fee.

Lunch: Point Pleasant Village Store.

157.0. Tohickon Creek enters, Pennsylvania side. Tohickon Creek is dam-controlled; in the spring and at dam releases, it contains Class III and IV rapids for kayakers and rafters. At other times Tohickon Creek is too shallow for any kind of boat. Gravel bars at the mouth of the creek extend almost to the middle of the river.

The main pumphouse for the Point Pleasant Diversion stands a few yards from the river near the mouth of Tohickon Creek. The pumphouse looks like a big, sturdy barn, and fits in well with the landscape. The actual intakes are inconspicuously located under the river. The Diversion pumps water from the Delaware to cool the nuclear power plant at Limerick, Pennsylvania. The Diversion was constructed in 1991, after lengthy controversy. Many local residents feared that the Diversion would draw so much water that recreational and fishing use of the Delaware would be diminished, but so far that has not proved to be so.

Map 30

156.9. River begins a wide turn to the left, entering Lower Black Eddy.

156.8. Numerous boat docks and swimming rafts for summer homes for next .4 mile, both sides. Many motorboats are active in this area. Canoeists should stay near the riverbanks.

156.1. Byram public access area, New Jersey, maintained by Delaware and Raritan Canal State Park, New Jersey State Park Service. There is a concrete boat ramp, ample parking, picnic tables, and privies. Carry-in/carry-out trash. Access from New Jersey Route 29.

156.0. Begin Bulls Island, New Jersey side. The channel between the New Jersey riverbank and Bulls Island leads to the Delaware and Raritan Feeder Canal. (See features section of this chapter.) By paddling down the channel, canoeists will reach the D&R Canal gate lock in .7 mile. There is a canoe launch and landing on the canal where the park road crosses. Canoes can be easily carried across Bulls Island from the canal to the river and vice versa.

155.9. The wings of Raritan Dam, also known as Lumberville Dam, extend from both banks to a gap in the middle of the river. The dam was originally constructed in the early 1800s to impound water for the Delaware and Raritan Feeder Canal, and has been renovated periodically.

The river flows through the gap at the center of the dam in a safe but very exciting Class I+ rapids. There is a precipitous drop-off, followed by standing waves up to 3 feet high.

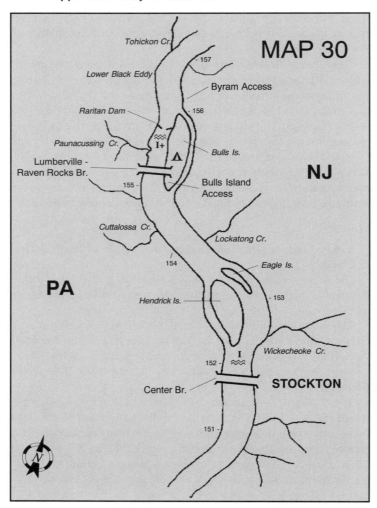

Water fails to go over the wing dams only when the river is very low. Canoeists should never attempt to go over the dams—there may be a potentially dangerous hydraulic at the base—but must pass through the center opening. To avoid passage through the Lumberville wing dam, canoeists may paddle down the channel on the New Jersey side of Bulls Island to the D&R Canal, then carry their boat across the island back to the river. But unless the river level is too high, by all means go through the dam—it's a great ride!

There is an unsupervised swimming area just upstream from the wing dam on the New Jersey side in the Bulls Island Recreation area.

The river below the wing dams is a favored fishing spot. Canoeists must take care not to interfere with anglers.

155.6. A Class I rapid with a few boulders. Paunacussing Creek enters, Pennsylvania side, with large gravel bars extending to the center of the river. The Delaware Canal (Pennsylvania side) crosses the creek in an aqueduct.

155.4. A rough dirt trail leads up the Pennsylvania riverbank to lock 12 on the Delaware Canal. There are picnic tables and fire grills at this site.

155.3. Pass under Lumberville–Raven Rocks Pedestrian Bridge, one of the most picturesque structures to span the Delaware. A wooden bridge was built at this site in 1853; it was condemned and closed in 1945. The present suspension bridge was built by John A. Roebling & Sons Company in 1947 on the original piers and abutments.

At the Pennsylvania end of the bridge stands a two-story stone house, built in 1853, which was used for many years by toll collectors. Immediately downstream from the bridge the famous Black Bass Hotel overlooks the canal and the river.

Lunch: Lumberville General Store, 100 yards south of pedestrian bridge.

155.2. Bulls Island access area, New Jersey, maintained by the New Jersey State Park Service, just downstream from the Lumberville–Raven Rocks bridge. There is a concrete boat ramp, ample parking, picnic areas, water, privies, trash disposal, and telephones. Access from New Jersey Route 29.

Camping. Bulls Island Recreation Area (R.D. 2, Box 417, Stockton, New Jersey 08559, 609-397-2949), operated by the New Jersey State Park Service. There are about 75 individual campsites nestled under the tall trees and along the river bank. Each site has a picnic table and firepit. There are new rest rooms with showers, a playground, and drinking water. The park office is located on the road leading to the Lumberville–Raven Rocks bridge. To reach the campsites most accessible from the river, canoes should be beached just upstream from the wing dam. This is the last public camping area on the Delaware.

35. The Lumberville–Raven Rocks pedestrian bridge, constructed in 1947. The Delaware Canal and towpath are in the foreground. Photo by the author.

155.0. A wide gravel bar extends from the downstream tip of Bulls Island.

154.8. The river begins wide turn to the left.

154.3. Cuttalossa Creek enters, Pennsylvania side.

153.9. Lockatong Creek enters, New Jersey side.

153.4. Begin Eagle Island in center of river.

There is a Class I rapids, with a few boulders, at the head of the left (New Jersey side) channel, and halfway down the channel between Eagle and Hendrick Islands.

153.3. Begin Hendrick Island, to the right of Eagle Island. The channel between the islands is passable, but the passage between Hendrick Island and the Pennsylvania side is very narrow and not navigable at low water level.

152.9. End Eagle Island.

152.8. Arched stone flood gates, New Jersey side, allow release of excess water from the D&R Feeder Canal.

152.4. Wickecheoke Creek enters, New Jersey side. Historic Smith's Mill, also known as Prallsville Mill, with its scenic spillway, can be seen at the mouth of the creek. A typical nineteenth-century gristmill, Smith's Mill is now part of D&R Canal State

36. Historic Prallsville Mill at Stockton, New Jersey, is now a center for art exhibits and music performances. Wickecheoke Creek joins the Delaware. Photo by the author.

Park, and is used as a center for arts and music. Concerts sponsored by the Delaware River Mill Society, the Delaware Riverkeeper, and other organizations are held at Prallsville Mill most summer Saturdays.

The railbed of the Belvidere-Delaware Railroad, completed in 1855 parallel to the D&R Canal, crosses Wickecheoke Creek on a steel trestle. The railbed is now an excellent bicycle and walking trail, maintained by the New Jersey State Park Service.

The last remaining covered bridge in New Jersey crosses Wickecheoke Creek about a mile from the Delaware.

152.2. End of Hendrick Island. A Class I rapids consisting of three submerged ledges with riffles in between. Watch for submerged and protruding boulders.

Author's note: On my 1996 trip from Hancock to Trenton, after successfully navigating Skinners Falls, Mongaup Rift, Foul Rift, Wells Falls, and every other rapids on the river, it was here that I came closest to an upset. The canoe caught sideways on a just-submerged rock and rolled hard—a reminder that the river is capable of reaching out and grabbing you anytime, anywhere.

Map 31

151.8. Pass under Center Bridge. This six-span crossing was constructed in 1926 on piers and abutments originally built in 1814. A wooden bridge built that year lasted until 1924, when it was destroyed by fire. This is the site of Reading's Ferry, which began regular crossings in 1711 and which was the first commercial ferry on the Delaware.

The community of Stockton, New Jersey, stands at the east end of the bridge.

Fast water under the bridge.

Lunch: Dilly's Ice Cream Corner, Pennsylvania end of Center Bridge; several casual restaurants in Stockton.

150.1. An unnamed creek enters, Pennsylvania side.

149.8. High-tension lines crackle overhead.

149.7. Pass under New Hope–Lambertville Toll Bridge, carrying U.S. Route 202. This bridge was completed in 1971.

149.6. Large gravel bar near Pennsylvania side.

149.5. Alexhauken Creek enters, New Jersey side. A large gravel bar extends one-quarter of the way across river.

Rabbit Run enters, Pennsylvania side.

Pass under power lines.

Enter Lambertville Eddy, extending to Wells Falls at Mile 148.0. Many motorboats and waterskiers use this eddy. Canoeists should stay near the sides.

148.8. Holcombe Island, New Jersey side, site of Lewis Shad Fishery and presently home to a local rowing club. Racing shells are stacked on racks near the river. Canoeists may use the private landing area (for access to Lambertville) at their own risk.

148.7. Pass under New Hope–Lambertville Bridge. A wooden bridge built at this site in 1814 was destroyed by the flood of 1903. The present six-span steel structure was built in 1904 on the original piers.

148.6–148.2. Shops, galleries, and restaurants of New Hope are close to water on Pennsylvania side.

148.6. Lambertville access area, New Jersey, maintained by New Jersey State Park Service and Delaware River Powerboat Association, extends about 100 yards along the New Jersey riverbank. There is a concrete boat ramp, parking, picnic tables, privies, and trash disposal.

Lunch: Many casual restaurants and other services may be found in both Lambertville and New Hope.

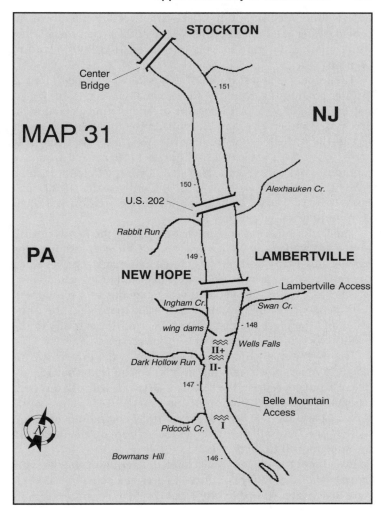

Features

The Delaware and Raritan Canal

In 1676 William Penn proposed the idea of connecting New York and Philadelphia by a canal across New Jersey. It was not until 1830, however, that the Delaware and Raritan Canal Company was chartered to construct the waterway. The canal opened to barge traffic in 1834, with tidewater locks on the Raritan River at New Brunswick and on the Delaware River at Bordentown. To provide water at a sufficient level for the canal at Trenton, a feeder canal was built along the Delaware River from Bulls Island to Trenton.

The feeder canal was not built as a waterway for boats, but as a water conduit. Even so, the feeder canal was navigable by canal barges and was an important means of transportation in Stockton, Lambertville, and Titusville in the nineteenth century. In the 1840s the locks at Lambertville were improved, allowing access from the Delaware River. Barges brought coal from the mountains of Pennsylvania, travelled down the Delaware Canal, crossed the river above Wells Falls, and entered the D&R Canal. From there coal could be barged to market at Trenton and other communities in central New Jersey.

The D&R Canal was constructed mostly by the hands of Irish immigrant workers. In 1832 a deadly epidemic swept through the labor camps. Many workers were buried in unmarked graves along the canal, with one mass grave at Bulls Island. The canal itself, which has already survived 150 years, remains as a monument to these laborers: the hand-laid rock walls that retain the canal water and the precision masonry of the canal locks testify to the quality workmanship that went into the canal.

The D&R Canal suffered the same fate as the other towpath canals in America, succumbing to competition from the more efficient railroads. Indeed, the Belvidere-Delaware Railroad was built parallel to the feeder portion of the canal in 1855. For a while the canal and railroad were operated under common ownership. In 1871 the Pennsylvania Railroad took a lease on the canal and operated it until the early 1930s.

Even though the D&R Canal closed to navigation after 99 years of barge traffic, it today continues to give valuable service. Delaware River water carried by the canal is sold to communities and industries throughout central New Jersey. Most of the water-control devices on the canal—locks, flumes, gates—have been modified for the canal's modern use as a water supply aqueduct. As a result, the D&R Canal continues to be maintained and is in excellent condition along its 60-mile length.

The D&R Feeder Canal closely parallels the Delaware River between the gate lock at Bulls Island and the Scudders Falls Bridge above Trenton. The towpath and canal are in excellent condition along the way. The canal is a fine place for beginning canoeists to practice and explore. Circle trips are possible by paddling downstream on the river, then returning upstream on the D&R Canal to the starting point. There are several low bridges and two locks which must be portaged around on the canal between Bulls Island and Scudders Falls.

Lambertville to Trenton

Mile 148.6 to 131.8 (16.8 miles)

This section begins with Wells Falls, the most severe rapids on the Delaware, and ends at Trenton Falls, which marks the boundary of tidewater. The river continues through the Piedmont geophysical province until Trenton Falls. Trenton Falls is on the "fall line," that is, the boundary between the Piedmont and the Coastal Plain provinces. Since the Piedmont is composed of solid rock and the Coastal Plain consists of uncemented sand and clay, the fall line causes severe rapids in many eastern rivers. The Great Falls of the Potomac near Washington, D.C., is a striking example. Below Trenton Falls the Delaware flows 133 miles through the Coastal Plain to the mouth of the river at Delaware Bay.

The lands along the river are increasingly urbanized in this section, starting with Lambertville and New Hope at the beginning, then Titusville, Washington Crossing, West Trenton, Yardley, Morrisville, and Trenton itself. Most of the way, however, the riverbank is lined with trees, and the scenery is not unpleasant. For the last mile above tidewater, the river is channelled between high concrete embankments.

At Wells Falls and Scudders Falls the river is funnelled through wing dams. Canoeists should never paddle over the dams, but should aim for the center chute. Wells Falls is so severe that novices are advised to detour the rapids on the D&R Canal (New Jersey) or the Delaware Canal (Pennsylvania). At extreme low tide the last ledges of Trenton Falls present hazardous rapids that should be avoided by all but the most experienced canoeists.

Pennsylvania Route 32 and New Jersey Route 29 parallel the river closely on either side. The Delaware Canal continues along the riverbank in Pennsylvania, in places swerving away from the river, while the D&R Canal in New Jersey is very near the river for the first 10 miles. Either canal makes for good circle trips by paddling down the river, then returning back upstream on the canal.

A turning point in the American Revolution took place on this section of the Delaware. On Christmas Day 1776, George Washington led his tired troops across the river for a surprise attack on the Hessian garrison at Trenton. Washington's victory revitalized the Revolutionary cause. Both New Jersey and Pennsylvania have established state parks to commemorate the event, and the two parks are well worth a visit.

Below Trenton the Delaware River is affected by the twice-daily surge of tides from the Atlantic Ocean. The river becomes much deeper and much more polluted. Oil tankers, freight barges, garbage scows, and other heavy shipping use the river for access to the industrial cities that line it. Though motorboating and sailing are popular in some areas, the Delaware below Trenton is not well suited for canoeing.

There are four public access areas in this section:

Lambertville Access (New Jersey), Mile 148.6
Belle Mountain (New Jersey), Mile 146.8
Yardley (Pennsylvania), Mile 138.7
Trenton Waterfront (New Jersey), Mile 131.8.

Except for a group campsite at Washington Crossing State Park, New Jersey, there are no public campgrounds in this section of the river. The riverbanks and islands are for the most part privately owned and developed. Trespassing is prohibited.

River Guide

Map 31

148.6. Lambertville access area, New Jersey, maintained by New Jersey State Park Service (D&R Canal State Park) and Delaware River Powerboat Association, extends about 100 yards along the New Jersey riverbank. There is a concrete boat ramp, parking, picnic tables, privies, and trash disposal.

148.5. Swan Creek enters, New Jersey side.

148.6–148.2. Shops, galleries, and restaurants of New Hope are close to water on Pennsylvania side.

148.2. Ingham Creek enters, Pennsylvania side.

148.1. Buoys advise "DANGER—DAM AHEAD."

148.0. Concrete wing dams extend from both sides to a chute in the center of the river. Canoeists should stop on either wing to reconnoiter—this is a potentially hazardous area. (See the description of Wells Falls in the features section of this chapter.)

Pass through the chute into Wells Falls, a Class II or III rapids (depending on the route and water level). There are 3- to 4-foot standing waves, dangerous ledges, and huge rocks. After the first drop at the chute, Class I+ rapids continue about 400 yards.

At normal water level, Wells Falls is easiest—merely Class II—on the left side; hidden ledges and enormous waves in the center and on the right make for Class III rapids.

147.6. Rapids peter out into short eddy, with large rocks protruding from the water on the Pennsylvania side.

147.4. Dark Hollow Run enters, Pennsylvania side.

146.8. Belle Mountain access, New Jersey, maintained by the New Jersey State Park Service (D&R Canal State Park) Constructed by the Young Adult Conservation Corps in 1980, there is a paved boat ramp, limited parking, carry-in/carry-out trash. Access from New Jersey Route 29.

The Golden Nugget Market Flea Market, with over 100 dealers of antiques and odds and ends for sale or trade, is located a short walk up New Jersey Route 29 from the access area.

Canoeists may hear the whistle of an old steam locomotive, an excursion train on the Black River & Western Railroad originating in Flemington, New Jersey.

146.6. Pidcock Creek enters, Pennsylvania side.

In the stone house near the mouth of Pidcock Creek, George Washington planned his 1776 assault on Trenton.

146.4. Class I rapids; watch for rocks.

Map 32

146.0. Keelers Island at New Jersey side; the channel to the left is normally too dry for passage.

Bowmans Tower can be seen atop the hill on the Pennsylvania side. (See description of Bowmans Hill in the features section of this chapter.)

145.1. Moores Creek enters via twin concrete arches, New Jersey side.

145.0. Belle Mountain Ski Area and a stone/gravel quarry, New Jersey side.

144.1. River bends slightly left.

144.0. Jericho Creek enters, Pennsylvania side.

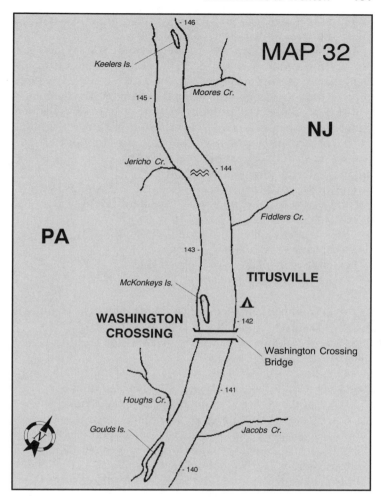

143.9. Enter Titusville Rift, an unobstructed riffle through the bend. Beware of shallows on the right.

143.1. The David Library of the American Revolution, open to the public, is located on Pennsylvania Route 32.

Fiddlers Creek enters via a stone arch, New Jersey side.

143.0–142.0. The community of Titusville, New Jersey, is situated on the bluffs, New Jersey side. There are many boat dock and swimming rafts along the riverbank.

142.3. McKonkeys Island, Pennsylvania. The channel along the Pennsylvania side is impassable at low water.

142.0. Washington Crossing State Parks, both sides; access is not developed, but it is easy to land a canoe for access to the picnic facilities, historic sites, and the like. (See description of Washington's Crossing in the features section of this chapter.)

141.8. Pass under Washington Crossing Bridge. A wooden bridge was built here in 1831, 55 years after Washington and his troops crossed in Durham boats on the way to Trenton. The present six-span steel truss bridge was completed in 1904 on the original masonry piers and abutments.

Lunch: Faherty's Deli, at New Jersey end of Washington Crossing Bridge; several shops and casual restaurants, Pennsylvania end of bridge.

Enter Scudders Eddy; slow water for next mile.

140.5. Jacobs Creek enters, New Jersey side.

Houghs Creek enters, Pennsylvania side.

Map 33

140.2. Goulds Island, Pennsylvania side. The right channel is too dry to canoe at low water.

140.0. Dyers Run enters, Pennsylvania side (behind Gould Island).

139.7. Enter Scudders Falls, a Class I+ rapid. Dilapidated concrete wing dams, covered with vegetation, extend from both sides to a chute at the center. At normal level river does not flow over dams. Canoeists should never go over the dams (there may be a dangerous hydraulic at foot of dams), but should pass through the chute in the center. Passage through the center chute is an unobstructed "V," with standing waves to about 2½ feet. "Only a drop and a rough race," in the words of J. Wallace Hoff.

Stay as far to the left (New Jersey side) as possible to go through a Class II rapids at a break in the wing dam. There is a steep drop into big standing waves, without any obstructions. Open canoes will almost surely ship water while passing through the chute.

The area below the dams is very popular with shad fishermen; canoeists must take care not to interfere with anglers.

139.5. Blackguard Island in center of river; the main channel is left, but the right channel is navigable and accessible through

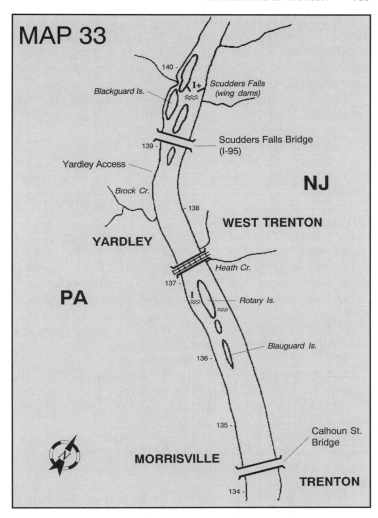

MAP 33

140 -

Blackguard Is.

I+ Scudders Falls
(wing dams)

Scudders Falls Bridge
(I-95)

139 -

Yardley Access

Brock Cr.

NJ

138

WEST TRENTON

YARDLEY

Heath Cr.

137 -

PA

Rotary Is.

Blauguard Is.

136 -

135 -

Calhoun St.
Bridge

MORRISVILLE

TRENTON

134 -

a chute near the right end of the dam.

The D&R Canal (Pennsylvania side) bends away from river and is no longer easily accessible.

139.1. Pass under Scudders Falls Bridge, carrying Interstate Route 95, completed in 1959.

139.0. Gravel bar in middle of channel.

138.7. Yardley access area, Pennsylvania, maintained by the

Pennsylvania Fish Commission. There is a wide paved ramp, parking, privies, and trash disposal. This is the last public access before tidewater and the urbanized areas of Trenton. All boats must bear a valid Pennsylvania boat registration. Access from Pennsylvania Route 32.

138.0. Brock Creek enters, Pennsylvania side. The Delaware Canal crosses the creek in a high aqueduct a short distance from the river.

A brownstone bridge abutment on the Pennsylvania side is all that remains of the old Yardley bridge, washed out in the great flood of 1955. Today a memorial to veterans occupies the bridge abutment.

Lunch: Several shops and casual restaurants may be found in the village of Yardley.

137.9. Lunch: Charcoal Steaks and Things, above a gravel landing area with riverside picnic tables, Pennsylvania side. Started as a smoky hot dog stand for boaters in the 1940s, Charcoal Steaks has ever since been known to locals as "Dirty Bill's."

137.3. Brownstone abutments of an old Pennsylvania Railroad bridge.

The multiple-arch Conrail bridge carries the West Trenton line that runs between New York and Philadelphia.

137.2. Gold Run enters, New Jersey side.

137.0. Rotary Island (formerly Park Island) begins in the center of the river: the main channel is left, but the right channel is navigable and includes a stretch of Class I rapids with rocks and ledges at Mile 136.6.

136.5. From left of the island a channel winds through overhanging trees of Rotary Island, impassable at low water.

136.3. A Class I rapid immediately at the end of Rotary Island flows left to right.

136.1. Blauguard Island begins in center of river; the island is submerged at moderately high water.

135.6–134.6. Holly Park, New Jersey side, parallels the river. There are playgrounds, picnic tables, and a physical-fitness course. This park originally extended all the way to tidewater, but the lower reaches were obliterated, amid some controversy, with improvements to New Jersey Route 29.

134.6. Rocks protrude from water, Pennsylvania side; easy maneuvering.

134.5. City of Morrisville waterworks, Pennsylvania side. There is an unimproved and unofficial access to the river, commonly used by anglers to launch boats. There is a gravel launch area and trash barrel.

134.4. Trenton City Waterworks intake, New Jersey side. Stay clear.

134.3. Pass under the Calhoun Street Bridge. A wooden bridge was built here in 1861 but was destroyed later by fire. The present seven-span steel truss was completed on the original piers and abutments in 1884, making it the second-oldest bridge across the Delaware (the Roebling Bridge at Lackawaxen, built in 1849, is the oldest). There have been recent plans to build a new bridge nearby and to preserve the Calhoun Street Bridge as a historic site for use by pedestrians and bicyclists.

Trenton, New Jersey, population 88,675 (1990), and Morrisville, Pennsylvania, stand at opposite ends of the bridge.

Map 34

134.1. Begin Trenton Falls, a Class I+ rapid extending nearly one mile. The main channel runs in the center of the river. Watch for numerous rocks and ledges on the right, impassable at normal water level.

There is a small island on the extreme left (New Jersey side). In the channel to the left of island is a small dam with a narrow chute, canoeable but not recommended. Water crests the dam when moderately high, and the chute may be hard to see. Beware of hydraulic!

134.0. Upper limit of tidewater; if the tide is high, the river is flat from here down.

133.9. The gold dome of the New Jersey state capitol, New Jersey side.

133.8. Assunpink Creek enters via a concrete channel, New Jersey side.

133.7. Ledges extend nearly across the river as the main channel winds through the center. A maze of ledges on the right (Pennsylvania side) may be navigated with some lifting and dragging.

133.5. Pass under the Bridge Street Bridge, also known as the "Trenton Makes" bridge because of south-facing lettering proclaiming "Trenton Makes, the World Takes." The first bridge to span the Delaware was built here in 1803–1806 upon the piers and abutments that support the present bridge. The bridge struc-

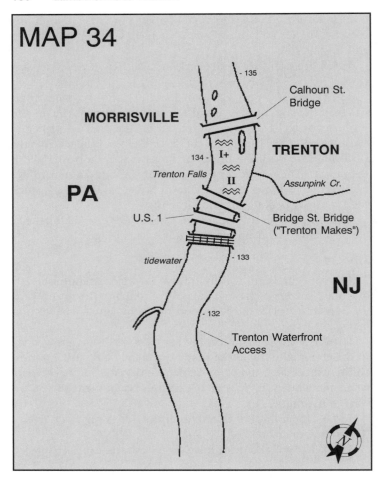

ture itself was remodeled repeatedly, at one time carrying a railroad as well as vehicle traffic, until the present five-span steel truss was completed in 1930.

At extreme low tide Trenton Falls becomes a potentially hazardous Class II rapids with high standing waves and boulders under the bridge in middle/left of river. The rapids can be avoided by maneuvering as far right as possible.

133.4. Pass under U.S. Route 1 toll bridge, built in 1952.

There is unimproved rough access under the bridge, Pennsylvania side.

37. The 1806 bridge at Trenton, the first span across the Delaware. The present-day "Trenton Makes" bridge stands on the piers and abutments that supported the original bridge. From a woodcut reprinted in John Cunningham, *New Jersey: America's Main Road* (1966).

The Route 1 bridge marks the limit of low tide.

133.3. Pass under the arched brownstone Amtrak mainline bridge, built in 1903.

133.2. Old Wharf fishing area, New Jersey side; operated by New Jersey Division of Fish, Game, and Shellfisheries. At one time a marine pier, there is no boat access.

132.7. Riverfront Park stadium, home of the minor-league baseball (AA) Trenton Thunder, stands close to the river on the New Jersey side. Long home runs to right field land in the river.

132.1. Trenton Marine Terminal, New Jersey side, once a deepwater port to the City of Trenton, today a city park.

131.8. Trenton Waterfront access area operated by the City of Trenton. Primarily intended for power boat and sailboat access to tidal waters, there are concrete ramps, wooden docks, ample parking, trash disposal, telephone, and rest rooms. Access from Lalor Street (New Jersey Route 29 South extension) on the south end of Trenton.

Features

New Hope, Pennsylvania

Located on the banks of the Delaware River, New Hope, Pennsylvania (population 1,473), is a small yet busy haven for artists, craftsmen, and tourists. It flourished as an industrial community

38. "Trenton Makes, the World Takes" (Bridge Street) Bridge at Trenton, New Jersey. Constructed on the site of the first-ever span across the Delaware (1806), this bridge marks the limit of tidewater and the end of the canoeable portion of the river. Photo by the author.

in the nineteenth century; however, the big mills have been converted into shops, offices, and condominium apartments, standing close to the Pennsylvania riverbank. New Hope today boasts 20 antique shops, 4 art galleries, nearly 100 specialty and gift shops, several night clubs (from sing-along piano bars to flashy discotheques), and more than 35 restaurants. There is an important regional theater, barge rides on the Delaware Canal, a steam train to Lahaska, and historical tours.

New Hope was founded in the early 1700s by John Wells, who operated a ferry across the river. Wells was also proprietor of the Old Ferry Tavern, now known as the Logan Inn (constructed in 1727). The growing community became first known as Coryells Ferry in honor of a subsequent ferry owner. In the late decades of the eighteenth century Benjamin Parry constructed and operated two mills. After the mills burned down in 1790, Parry rebuilt them and optimistically called them the "New Hope Mills." The name stuck, and the community itself soon became known as New Hope.

Virtually all of New Hope is within easy walking distance of the Delaware River. The entire town is squeezed onto four streets, two alleys, and a towpath. The summer crowds are convivial, and the atmosphere day or night is captivating.

The village's special attractions include:

1. The Parry Mansion, at the corner of South Main and Ferry Streets, open to the public to view the antique architecture, furnishings, and household items.
2. Mule barges take daily summer excursions 4½ miles along the Delaware Canal, departing hourly from the barge landing on the towpath just south of the center of town.
3. The Bucks County Playhouse, on South Main Street, features evening performances of well-known musicals.
4. A reconstructed Coryell's Ferry plies the Delaware River from its base between South Main Street and the riverbank.
5. The New Hope and Ivyland Steam Railroad leaves several times a day from the depot near the canal at Bridge Street and tours 16 miles through the Bucks County countryside to Lahaska and back.

Lambertville, New Jersey

Like New Hope on the other side of the river, Lambertville began as a ferry town, grew as a canal port, and burgeoned as a regional industrial center. Today, although most of Lambertville's industry is gone, the town is enjoying a renewal as a center of art, culture, and historical renovation.

The first permanent settler in Lambertville was one John Holcombe, who arrived in 1705. By 1770 Well's Ferry regularly plied between New Jersey and Pennsylvania. The little community became known as Coryells Ferry in 1770 when Emanuel Coryell superseded John Wells. (A restored Coryell's ferry operates today out of New Hope as a tourist attraction.)

Lambertville acquired its present name in 1814 when John Lambert, a United States senator from New Jersey, arranged for his nephew's appointment as postmaster. With the construction of the Delaware and Raritan (D&R) Canal in the 1830s and the Belvidere and Delaware Railroad in 1851, Lambertville developed into an important regional commercial center. Ample water power was available at Wells Falls, and mills were constructed for grist, paper, cotton, India rubber, saw timber, and iron works.

Just as railroads ultimately forced the closing of the D&R Canal, factories in the Midwest and in big eastern cities proved too fierce competition for the mills of Lambertville. The town declined economically, and there has been little new construction since the turn of the century.

Today Lambertville is being revived as a residential and cultural community. The citizens of Lambertville are proud of their heritage and actively promote historical preservation and restoration. Many of the old brick row houses have been renovated into modern artistic homes. Lambertville's Acme market has been featured in *Smithsonian Magazine* as a surviving example of art deco architecture. The long-abandoned railroad depot, built in 1880, has been recently reopened as a fine restaurant.

With a population of less than 5,000, Lambertville is not a large city. Yet many services and a variety of stores are available and easily accessible from the river. There are numerous cafes and restaurants, antique shops, boutiques, and grocery stores. The Lambertville House, a hotel-restaurant open to the public since 1812, stands just at the end of the Lambertville–New Hope Bridge. The restored Lambertville Station restaurant is across the street.

Wells Falls

There has always been a rapid at Wells Falls, which is named for the operator of an early ferry between Lambertville and New Hope. In 1812 wing dams were constructed to impound water for mill power, and so the river was confined to a narrow chute in the middle. The dam has been rebuilt and upgraded repeatedly, most recently in 1968.

Wells Falls was one of the most difficult passages on the river for timber raftsmen in the eighteenth and nineteenth centuries. Local entrepreneurs familiar with the rapid made a good living by piloting rafts through Wells Falls, for a fee of as much as five dollars per raft. The pilots became so familiar with the passage that every rock was known to them by name: "100-barrel Rock" (a Durham boat carrying 100 barrels of flour could pass when water covered this rock); "Foamer"; "Dram Rock"; "Buckwheat Ledge"; and "Rodmans Rocks," named for a raftsman who was wrecked and drowned at the site. The flow of the river has been changed so drastically by the wing dams that the exact locations of these obstacles are no longer known.

A buoy half a mile downstream from the old New Hope–Lambertville Bridge warns "Danger—Falls ahead—200 feet." Wells Falls is indeed the most severe rapid on the Delaware River, the only one measured above Class II by the DRBC.

One warm summer day in 1981 the severity of the rapid was tragically proved. The river level was normal, and flow was confined to the chute between the wings. Half a dozen kayakers, wearing helmets and PFDs, challenged the wavefront breaking around the lip of the dam, trying to hold a stationary position on the wave, balancing current and gravity. People in rubber rafts bounced over and through the 3-foot haystacks where the river concentrates its momentum just past the dam. Several canoeists stopped at the dam to reconnoiter their path through the rapids.

Then a lone canoe approached, bearing three passengers. They were headed straight through, without stopping to learn the course. They wore no life jackets. The sternman sat not on the seat but high on the rear deck, sipping from a can of beer or soda. The circumstances invited disaster.

The canoe sped through the chute, glanced off a rock, then rolled and swamped in the second haystack, pitching its occupants into the rapid. The three canoeists bobbed downriver, their boat, paddles, and persons separating in the rocks and crosscurrents. Some of the kayakers, seeing that the men were in trouble, paddled vigorously to the rescue. Two of the canoeists were pulled to safety, but the third could not be reached in time. His body was recovered by kayakers 15 minutes after the spill, and all attempts at reviving him were in vain. The hard lessons of river safety had been demonstrated once again.

Even for proficient canoeists Wells Falls represents a challenge. At normal water level, all the river rushes through the narrow chute between low wing dams extending from both banks. A great boulder, nearly submerged, lurks in the center of the chute just past the opening. The "V" of the main current flows in a very narrow channel to the right of the boulder, moving slightly left, with haystacks at three to four feet high. A canoe almost certainly will take on water in a run of these waves, making for sluggish maneuvering around the rocks below.

It is possible to "sneak" Wells Falls at the extreme left side of the chute: the canoeist must make a very quick turn into the eddy behind the New Jersey wing, then negotiate between numerous small ledges and through narrow channels. This course is tricky, but the current is not so overwhelming as in the main channel.

When the river is high enough to flow over the dams, Wells Falls probably cannot be handled in an open canoe. The haystacks grow to five or six feet, and submerged boulders hardly can be detected in the muddy flow. Canoeists should never attempt to go *over* the dams; the powerful hydraulic at the foot would easily trap a canoe and its occupants.

For those who allow valor to yield to discretion and determine that Wells Falls is beyond their capabilities, there are two very attractive alternatives to running the main channel of the rapids. A canoe can be easily carried over either of the wing dams and placed into the eddy below; the route requires some maneuvering but avoids the severe current and waves encountered by passage through the chute. Or, canoeists may portage a few yards to the D&R Canal on the New Jersey riverbank, paddle down the canal, then transfer back to the river below the falls.

Wells Falls is an exciting challenge for experienced canoeists. Safety precautions are essential: reconnoiter the route by stopping on either wing of the dam, securely fastening PFDs, and wearing a helmet, if available, is advisable. After running the rapid, canoeists can beach on the New Jersey side and haul their boats up to the D&R Canal. It is a fairly easy paddle back upstream to the Lambertville access area with a short portage around a lock.

Bowmans Hill

Anytime during the spring, summer, and early fall wild flowers are plentiful all along the Delaware River. The riverside habitat is home to many species, and fields and forests just beyond the banks offer a niche to many more varieties. But at Bowmans Hill Wild Flower Preserve, part of Pennsylvania's Washington Crossing State Park about 2 miles south of New Hope, a score of different habitats has been preserved and cultivated, providing visitors an opportunity to observe and study most of the common—and not so common—varieties of wild flowers found in this part of the country.

In the 1930s the Council for the Preservation of Natural Beauty sponsored the establishment of a wild flower preserve at the base of Bowmans Hill. In those early years volunteers and workers of the Works Progress Administration (WPA) cut trails, thinned undergrowth, drained and made swamps, and enhanced or established the range of habitats present today at the wild flower preserve. In the 1960s a headquarters was built to be used as an education and research center and to house collections and exhibits. Today the Bowmans Hill Wild Flower Preserve Association, together with the Pennsylvania State Park Service, continues to maintain and encourage the growth of wild flowers in the preserve.

Bowmans Hill Wild Flower Preserve is spread over a 100-acre tract along Pidcock Creek. More than 20 wild flower trails are arranged through the preserve: each takes the visitor through a different habitat and presents a different array of blossoms. "Penn's Woods" (where most of the species of trees native to Pennsylvania may be found), the marsh marigold trail, azaleas at the bridge, the sphagnum trail, the barrens, the medicinal trail, and 15 others await exploration by visitors.

Many of the trail habitats were present before the wild flower preserve was established; others were specially and carefully developed by importing soils, modifying moisture conditions, and varying exposures to sunlight. The maintenance of Bowmans Hill Wild Flower Preserve requires considerable expertise in the propagation and cultivation of plants that normally grow only in the wild and are often quite resistant to human interference. Wild plant propagation and cultivation are attempted constantly at the preserve, often with success but sometimes not. Wild plant propagation is a tricky business; each species has its own set of conditions that must be met before it can thrive. Very often these conditions are not known, so good guesswork and trial and error play a major role in the work at the wild flower preserve. Seed preparation, germination time (as much as four years!), amount and frequency of watering, temperature, acidity, nutrients, air supply, exposure to light, and soil all must be just so for wild flowers to prosper. The wild flower preserve has some excellent displays on wild plant propagation, and experiments may be seen throughout the preserve.

Throughout the year, but especially during the summer months, the wild flower preserve sponsors events for members of the association and for the public. On almost every summer Sunday there is a family nature walk: a guided tour of selected habitats of the preserve. Recently Wednesdays have been volunteer day; the public is invited to assist in the operation and maintenance of the preserve. This assistance might include collecting and sorting seeds, maintaining trails, and helping with the propagation of wild flowers. The preserve also sponsors special classes in horticulture and in wild flower propagation. A complete calendar of events is available from the preserve headquarters building. The headquarters building is open every day of the year, except major holidays, from 9:00 A.M. to 5:00 P.M. In addition to wild flower exhibits the headquarters building contains the Platt collection of bird nests, eggs, and mounted specimens.

The wild flower preserve is not the only attraction of Bowmans Hill. At the summit of the hill stands Bowmans Tower, erected in 1930. For a modest fee, visitors can ride an elevator to the top to view the Delaware Valley and surrounding countryside. Bowmans Hill was used as an observation point by Washington's army in preparation for the Christmas night crossing in 1776. At the base of the hill and along the river are the Thompson-Neely House (built in 1702), the restored Thompson Gristmill, and the graves of Revolutionary soldiers.

Bowmans Hill is accessible from the river on the Pennsylvania side about a half mile downstream from the Belle Mountain access area. Canoes may be landed near the mouth of Pidcock Creek at River Mile 146.2. A large picnic pavilion stands on the riverbank just upstream from Pidcock Creek.

Washington's Crossing

Washington's crossing of the Delaware on Christmas night in 1776 and the ensuing battle of Trenton reversed the momentum of the American Revolution. Until then, Washington's army had suffered a series of defeats and retreats; the morale of the troops was at rock bottom. Enlistments were over on December 31, and most of the soldiers wanted to go home. The Revolutionary cause seemed hopeless.

At this crucial time, Washington and a division of 2,400 men were camped in the cold forest of Bucks County. A garrison of 1,400 trained Hessian mercenaries was quartered eight miles downstream at Trenton. Washington daringly planned a surprise attack on the Hessian garrison late on Christmas night; the Americans desperately needed this victory. Stealth was the essence of the operation. Daniel Bray, an officer in the Continental Army, commandeered a small armada of Durham boats and flat-bottom ferries from

39. On Christmas night of 1776, Washington crossed the Delaware to attack the Hessian garrison in Trenton. Washington's victory revitalized the American Revolution. This statue is in Washington Crossing Historic Park, Pennsylvania. Photo by the author.

up and down the river, securing them near McKonkeys Island.

Christmas night at Trenton was cold, with blowing sleet and snow. The river was choked with an unusual amount of ice. From the Pennsylvania banks just upstream from the present-day Washington Crossing Bridge, the American soldiers poled and rowed to the New Jersey side. The crossing took almost nine hours, much longer than Washington had planned. After the troops were assembled, Washington led a quick march eight miles to Trenton. The Hessians were completely surprised and conquered with few casualties. As word of Washington's victory spread throughout the colonies, new hope was breathed into the American cause.

The states of Pennsylvania and New Jersey have commemorated Washington's crossing of the Delaware by the establishment of two state parks. On the Pennsylvania side, a cluster of Revolutionary-era homes, barns, and shops may be toured. McKonkey Ferry Inn, where Washington and his aides dined before the crossing, stands at the access to the bridge. The boat house shelters reproductions of the famous Durham boats, which were used during the crossing and to haul cargo along the Delaware River for many years. The highlight of a visit to the park is a reproduction of Emanuel Leutze's famous painting of Washington crossing the Delaware (ironically, the original was destroyed by allied bombing of Germany during World War II). The painting is located in a visitors' center theater, and it is the focus of a dramatization of the events of 1776. There are two large picnic areas with rest rooms.

Washington Crossing State Park, New Jersey, established in 1912, is considerably more extensive than its sister park across the river. There are four picnic areas with tables, pavilions, rest rooms, and grills, and many acres of open space for picnicking. Among the best of these spots is a grassy strip just atop the riverbank extending several hundred yards upstream from the bridge. The visitors' center, opened in 1976, features the Swan collection of the American Revolution. The Swan family has assembled an impressive display of Revolutionary firearms, swords, uniforms, letters, maps, money, and nearly every other artifact imaginable. An electronic map and slide show tell the story of Washington's army in 1776.

Russell Hoover's remarkable painting of Washington crossing the Delaware is also on prominent display at the visitors' center. This painting, more historically accurate than the more famous work displayed in Pennsylvania, hung for many decades in a darkened stairwell in the Trenton Public Library before it was rediscovered in 1982.

Another feature of the park is the George Washington Memorial Arboretum, which contains more than 80 species of trees and shrubs. The New Jersey State Forest Nursery is also here, where many varieties of trees are propagated for planting on public and private lands throughout the state. There is also a nature center and natural area, and numerous ballfields and play areas.

The Open Air Theater is one of the highlights of New Jersey's Washington Crossing State Park. Sponsored by the Washington Crossing Association of New Jersey, local theater groups perform on a stage in the center of a natural amphitheater. There is a performance almost every night in the summer.

Washington's crossing of the Delaware is reenacted, complete with troops in Revolutionary uniforms and Durham boats, every

Christmas afternoon. Thousands of spectators line the bridge and New Jersey and Pennsylvania riverbanks to witness this annual event. On the Fourth of July, the community of Titusville sponsors a fireworks display over the river.

Washington Crossing State Park is accessible from the river on either shore immediately upstream from the Washington Crossing Bridge. All park facilities are within walking distance of the river. There is easy canoe landing, but the riverbanks are steep. Access is not developed.

Trenton, New Jersey

The sign on the bridge between Trenton, New Jersey, and Morrisville, Pennsylvania, boldly states, "Trenton Makes, the World Takes." Trenton has long been an important manufacturing center. One of its earliest products was ceramics, which continues to be an important industry in Trenton; Lenox fine china and American Standard plumbing fixtures remain headquartered in Trenton. Roebling Steel began manufacturing wire cables for suspension bridges in Trenton in 1848, and the Roebling Company remains there today. Other plants in Trenton produce rubber goods, fabrics, electrical parts, and other commodities.

In 1679 Quaker Mahlon Stacy built a house and gristmill at "Ye Ffalles of Ye De La Warr." William Trent, a merchant from Philadelphia, purchased some of Stacy's land and divided it for sale in 1714. "Trent's town" grew as it attracted commerce from the upper Delaware. In 1727 a ferry began operations to convey passengers across the Delaware on their way between New York City and Philadelphia. The first bridge to span the Delaware was built at Trenton. In 1798, as burgeoning traffic overwhelmed ferry operations, the New Jersey legislature authorized construction of "a good and permanent bridge across the river Delaware . . . to facilitate travel between this and Southern States." The bridge, constructed of five wooden arches over four massive stone pillars, was opened with "elaborate exercises" on January 30, 1806. The foundations of the first bridge were well-laid; the present-day "Trenton Makes" bridge stands on the piers and abutments built in 1806.

The United States Congress met in Trenton in 1784, and for a while considered making Trenton the capital of the new nation. Trenton is the capital city of New Jersey. The gold dome of the statehouse is clearly visible from the Delaware River. Other government buildings are clustered in the capital complex that rises above the river, including Labor and Industry, Health and Agriculture, and the new Richard Hughes Justice Center.

There are numerous historic buildings and sites in Trenton, most of them easily accessible from the Delaware River. William Trent's home, built in 1719, is open as a museum not far from the Bridge Street Bridge. The Old Barracks, built in 1758, housed many of the Hessian officers captured in Washington's raid. The Old Barracks is open as a museum and may be found just below the statehouse. Across the street is the old Masonic lodge, built in 1793.

The state library, the state museum, and the domed planetarium are located close to the river just below the Calhoun Street Bridge. The museum contains fascinating permanent exhibits of the natural and cultural history of New Jersey. Special art exhibits change every few months. The planetarium has several shows daily.

Parts of the old industrial city of Trenton have fallen into urban decay. But the community is making great efforts to refurbish these areas, and citizens of Trenton are proud of their heritage. The whole city turns out for the annual heritage days festival, held during the first weekend of June, for a smorgasbord of activities, arts and crafts, and ethnic foods.

There are, of course, many stores and services in Trenton, but for the most part these are not near the Delaware River. Canoeists seeking supplies are advised to look in Morrisville, Pennsylvania, near the Calhoun Street and Bridge Street crossings.

Appendixes

Important Contacts

National Park Service

Delaware Water Gap National Recreation Area

Twenty-four-hour emergency phone: 717-588-2435 or 800-543-HAWK

Park Headquarters
Bushkill, PA 18324
717-588-2451

Dingmans Falls (PA) visitors center
717-828-7802

Kittatinny Point (NJ) visitors center
908-496-4458

Upper Delaware Scenic and Recreational River
24-hour emergency phone: 717-559-7527

Park Headquarters
RR 2 Box 2428
Beach Lake, PA 18405-9737
717-729-7135

Superintendent
P.O. Box C
Narrowsburg, NY 12764
717-729-8251

Interpretive Office
Lackawaxen, PA
717-685-4871

Information Center
Narrowsburg, NY 12764
914-252-3947

South District Ranger Office (the Coop)
Barryville, NY
914-557-0222

South District Ranger Office
Shohola, PA
717-559-7527

North District Ranger Office
Milanville, PA
717-729-7862

River Information Line (recorded report of river
and weather conditions)
914-252-7100

State of New York

New York Department of Environmental Conservation

50 Wolf Road
Albany, NY 12233-4790
518-457-3521

NY-DEC Regional Office, Reg. 3 (Sullivan and Orange Counties)

21 S. Putt Corners Road
New Paltz, NY 12561-1696
914-256-3000

NY-DEC Regional Office, Reg. 4 (Delaware County)

Route 10, Jefferson Road
Stamford, NY 12167-1696
607-652-7364

State of New Jersey

New Jersey Department of Environmental Protection

Division of Parks and Forestry
Box CN 404
Trenton, NJ 08625-0404
609-292-2797

Division of Fish, Game, and Wildlife
Box CN 400
Trenton, NJ 08625-4000
609-292-2965

Northern Region Field Office
908-725-8240

Delaware and Raritan Canal State Park
625 Canal Road
Somerset, NJ 08873
908-873-3050

Bulls Island Recreation Area
2185 Daniel Bray Highway
Stockton, NJ 08559
609-397-2949

High Point State Park
Box 1480, Route 23
Sussex, NJ 07461
201-875-4800

Stokes State Forest
1 Coursen Road
Branchville, NJ 07826
201-948-3820

Washington Crossing State Park
355 Washington Crossing Road
Titusville, NJ 08560
609-737-0623

Worthington State Forest
HC 62 Box 2
Columbia, NJ 07832
908-841-9575

Commonwealth of Pennsylvania

Pennsylvania Department of Environmental Resources

Bureau of State Parks
P.O. Box 8551
Harrisburg, PA 17105-8551
800-637-2757

Pennsylvania Fish and Boat Commission
Boat Registration Division
P.O. Box 68900
Harrisburg, PA 17106-8900
717-657-4551

Pennsylvania Fish and Boat Commission
Fish Division
P.O. Box 67000
Harrisburg, PA 17106-7000
717-657-4518

Pennsylvania Fish and Boat Commission
Northeast Region
P.O. Box 88
Sweet Valley, PA 18656
717-477-5717

Pennsylvania Game Commission
Northeast Region
P.O. Box 220
Dallas, PA 18612-0220
717-675-1143
800-228-0789

Pennsylvania Bureau of Forestry
Northeast Region (camping permits)
717-424-3001

Hugh Moore Canal Museum and Park
200 S. Delaware Drive
P.O. Box 877
Easton, PA 18044-0877
610-250-6700

Delaware Canal State Park
11 Lodi Hill Road
Upper Black Eddy, PA 18972
610-982-5560

Washington Crossing State Historic Park
P.O. Box 107
Washington Crossing, PA 18977
215-493-4076

Other

Appalachian Trail Conference
P.O. Box 807
Harpers Ferry, WV 25425
304-535-6331

Delaware Riverkeeper
P.O. Box 356
Washington Crossing, PA 18977-0326
215-369-1188 / 800-8-DELAWAR

Upper Delaware Council
211 Bridge Street
P.O. Box 217
Narrowsburg, NY 12764-6404
914-252-3022

Delaware River Basin Commission
P.O. Box 7360
West Trenton, NJ 08628
609-882-9500

Canoe Rental/Livery Services

The following businesses offer canoes and other craft for rental use on the Delaware River. All information has been provided by the operators.

Adventure Sports
P.O. Box 175
Marshalls Creek, PA 18335
717-223-0505 / 800-487-2628

Two miles north of I-80 Exit 52, on Route 209 in Marshalls Creek. April through October. Canoe and raft rentals with shuttle transportation for trips through the Delaware Water Gap National Recreation Area. Guided, outfitted, and provisioned trips available.

Bucks County River Country (Point Pleasant Canoe and Tube)
2 Walters Lane
Point Pleasant, PA 18950
215-297-5000 / FAX: 215-297-5643

Eight miles north of New Hope on PA Route 32 in Bucks County, PA; near Philadelphia, 90 minutes from New York City. April 15 (tubes May 15) through September 30. Canoe trips, one- to five-day duration. Transportation to all access points.

Cedar Rapids Kayak and Canoe Outfitters
P.O. Box 219
Barryville, NY 12719
914-557-8218

Eighteen miles north of Port Jervis on NY Route 97; 25 miles from Monticello, NY. Canoe, kayak, raft, and tube rentals, with transportation to all points Hancock to Port Jervis. Campground and riverfront restaurant at base.

Chamberlain Canoes, Rafts and Tubes
P.O. Box 155, River Road
Minisink Acres Mall
Minisink Acres, PA 18314
800-422-6631

River Road one mile from I-80 Exit 53 at Delaware Water Gap. May through October 20. Reservations recommended. Canoe, raft, and tube rentals with transportation. Overnight river camping trips in the Delaware Water Gap National Recreational Area. Personal canoes portaged. Group eco-tours of Delaware River available.

Doe Hollow Boat Rentals
1770 Riverton Road
Bangor, PA 18013
610-498-2193

On Riverton Road, one mile north of Belvidere Bridge. Canoe, tube, and rowboat rentals.

Hankins House
P.O. Box 127
Hankins, NY 12741
914-887-4423

Five miles west of Callicoon on NY Route 97. Reservations recommended. Canoe and tube rentals, transportation available. Hotel, restaurant, and tavern at base.

Kittatinny Canoes
HC 67 Box 360
Dingmans Ferry, PA 18328
800-356-2852

Canoe, kayak, raft, and tube rentals with transportation from four bases. Monthly "learn to canoe" days, wild flower and wildlife tours, fall foliage tours. April through October. Reservations recommended.
Barryville, NY: 2½ miles north of Barryville on NY Route 97.
Pond Eddy, NY: 3 miles north of Pond Eddy on NY Route 97.
Milford, PA: U.S. Route 209, 3 miles north of Milford.
Dingmans Ferry: Pennsylvania end of Dingmans Bridge.
Canoe launch also available at public access sites. Camping at Barryville base and at Riverbeach Campsites, Milford, PA.

Landers River Trips
1336 Route 97
Narrowsburg, NY 12764
800-252-3925

Main office (Ten Mile River Lodge) on NY Route 97, 3 miles south of Narrowsburg. April through October. Reservations recommended. Canoe, raft, kayak, and tube rentals from 10 locations, Hancock to Port Jervis. Special events throughout the season. Camping at four riverfront campgrounds, motel.

Pack Shack Adventures
P.O. Box 127, 88 Broad Street
Delaware Water Gap, PA 18327
717-424-8533 / 800-424-0955

Exit 53 off I-80, on Route 611 next to Shell minimart. April 1 through November 1. Reservations recommended. Canoes, kayaks, rafts, tube, and camping gear rentals, sales, and service. Guided/outfitted trips from one to five days. Transportation to and from all access points Port Jervis to Martins Creek. Specializing in scout trips and groups.

Pleasant Valley Campsite and Canoe Rentals
RR 1 Box 8A
Equinunk, PA 18417
717-224-4083

Two miles south on PA Route 1023 from Route 91 at Equinunk store. May 15 through October 1. Canoe rentals and transportation, Hancock to Lordville.

Red Barn Campground and Canoe Rental
P.O. Box 159
Hankins, NY 12741
914-887-4995

NY Route 97, 5 miles north of Callicoon. Canoe and tube rentals.

Silver Canoe Rentals
37 South Maple Avenue
Port Jervis, NY 12771
914-856-7055 / 800-724-8342

Close to I-84, NJ Route 23, U.S. Route 209. 90 minutes from New York City area. Bus and train services nearby. Mid-April through September 30. Reservations recommended. Canoe trips, raft trips, and tubing, with transportation, from Pond Eddy to Port Jervis or Port Jervis to Milford, PA.

Soaring Eagle Campsite and Canoe Livery
RR 1 Box 300
(Kellams Bridge)
Equinunk, PA 18417
717-224-4666

PA Route 1018, 6 miles from PA Route 191 (at Kellams Bridge). April 15 through October 15. Reservations recommended. Canoe and tube trips, with portage from Hancock to Narrowsburg.

T & W Rentals
Box 1796, RD 1
Route 46
Columbia, NJ 07832
908-475-4608

On U.S. Route 46, 10 miles south of Delaware Water Gap, 4 miles north of NJ Route 31. May through September. Reservations recommended. Canoe, tube, and raft rental. Transportation up river, one way only. Island campsites available at base camp.

Tri-State Canoe and Boar Rental
Box 400, Shay Lane
Matamoras, PA 18336
717-491-4948 / 800-56-CANOE

April 15 through October 15. Reservations strongly recommended. Canoe, kayak, raft, tube, and rowboat rentals; day or multi-day canoe trips, leisure or white water; transportation of private boats; guided moonlight raft trips and barbeque. Camping at Matamoras base.
Matamoras, PA: off I-84 at PA exit 11, off Route 6/209 near the Best Western hotel.
Pond Eddy, NY: NY Route 97 one mile south of Pond Eddy bridge.

Two River Junction Float Trips
1 Scenic Drive, Box 1A
Lackawaxen, PA 18435
717-685-2010

Located in Lackawaxen, PA, just north of Roebling Bridge and Zane Grey museum. May through September. Canoes, rafts, kayaks, and tubes, with transportation from Hancock to Lackawaxen; guided fishing, hunting, and sightseeing trips available.

Whitewater Willie's
17 West Main Street
Port Jervis, NY 12771
914-856-2229 / 800-233-RAFT

Port Jervis, NY: Access off I-84, at terminus of NY Route 97. Mid-April through mid-October, weather permitting. Reservations strongly recommended. Canoeing, rafting, and tubing; free transportation to Pond Eddy and Mongaup bases; guided trips available.

Wild and Scenic River Tours
166 Route 97
Barryville, NY 12719
800-836-0366

On NY Route 97, 1 mile north of Route 55 (Barryville/Shohola bridge). Weekends April through June and September through October, daily July through August. Self-guided canoe, raft, kayak, and tube trips with professional instruction. Transportation between Barryville base and select access points. Riverfront campsites for boating customers, local lodging at guest houses arranged.

Camping on the Delaware

Camping along the Delaware River is permitted for a fee at many commercial and public campgrounds. In addition, camping is permitted without charge (one night only) at several unimproved campsites near the river and on river islands within the Delaware Water Gap National Recreation Area. From north to south, commercial and public campgrounds on the Delaware are listed below. Unless otherwise noted, all campgrounds have running water and restrooms. All information has been provided by the operators.

Mile 323.0 (approx.): Pleasant Valley Campsite (RR 1 Box 8A, Equinunk, PA 18417, 717-224-4083). On PA Route 1023 (Pine Mill Road) 2 miles south of Route 191, at Equinunk store. Campsite is about 2 miles from river. Tent sites, showers, laundry.

Mile 312.7: Soaring Eagle Campsite and Canoe Livery (RR 1 Box 300 [Kellams Bridge], Equinunk, PA 18417, 717-224-4666). PA Route 1018, 6 miles from PA Route 191 (at Kellams Bridge). April 15 through October 15; reservations recommended. Twenty riverfront tent campsites, hot showers, flush toilets, firepits, picnic tables.

Mile 310.0: Red Barn Campground (P.O. Box 159, Hankins, NY 12741, 914-887-4995). Route 97 5 miles north of Callicoon. May 1 through October 15. Riverfront tent sites, showers, laundry, store.

Mile 295.4: Skinners Falls Campground (c/o Landers River trips, 1336 Route 97, Narrowsburg, NY 12764, 914-252-3925 / 800-252-3925). Located at NY end of Milanville–Skinners Falls Bridge. Tent sites and lean-tos, camp store, showers. Campers must be using Landers or privately owned river craft.

Mile 290.2: Narrowsburg Campground (c/o Landers River Trips 1336 Route 97, Narrowsburg, NY 12764, 914-252-3925 / 800-252-3925). Located on the bluffs just upstream of the Narrowsburg Bridge. Tent sites and lean-tos, camp store, showers. Campers must be using Landers or privately owned river craft. The community of Narrowsburg is accessible from this campground.

Mile 278.5: Ascalona Campground (Route 97, Minisink Ford, NY 12719, 914-557-6554). NY Route 97, 2 miles north of Roebling Bridge. Riverside tent sites, privies, picnic tables.

Mile 275.6: Minisink Campground, c/o Landers River Trips (1336 Route 97, Narrowsburg, NY 12764, 914-252-3925 / 800-252-3925). NY Route 97 about 2.5 miles north of Barryville. Riverside tent sites and lean-tos, showers, camp store. Campers must be using Landers or privately owned river craft.

Mile 275.5: Indian Head Canoes (Route 97, Barryville, NY 12719, 914-557-9777 / 800-874-2628). Riverfront tent sites and lean-tos at Indian Head Canoes base.

Mile 275.4: Kittatinny Campgrounds (Route 97, Box 95, Barryville, NY 18337, 914-557-8611 or -8004). NY Route 97 2 miles north of Barryville. River- and streamfront campsites, showers, swimming pool, deli and grill, camp store. Customers of Kittatinny Canoes river trips have priority for campsites. Campers going on the river must use Kittatinny or private canoes only.

Mile 275.2: Cedar Rapids Kayak and Canoe Outfitters (P.O. Box 219, Barryville, NY 12719, 914-557-8218). Eighteen miles north of Port Jervis on NY Route 97. Camping on riverfront sites at Cedar Rapids Inn. Hot showers, restaurant, and bar.

Mile 274.5: Wild and Scenic River Tours (166 Route 97, Barrryville, NY 12719, 914-557-8723 / 800-836-0366). Tent sites on the river at Wild and Scenic's canoe base.

Mile 273.2: Shohola Campground (RR #1, Box 959, Shohola, PA 18458-9704, 717-559-7819). One and a quarter miles up Bee Hollow Road, Shohola. Seasonal campers only.

Mile 267.3: Jerrys Three Rivers Canoes (P.O. Box 7, Pond Eddy, NY 12770, 914-557-6078). Jerrys has riverfront tent sites and lean-tos at its canoe base just north of the Pond Eddy bridge.

Mile 266: Indian Head Canoes (Route 97, Barryville, NY 12719, 914-557-8777 / 800-874-2628). Tent sites and lean-tos at Indian Head's Pond Eddy canoe base.

Mile 262.9: Buckhorn Natural Area: primitive camping on PA State Forest lands, by permit only. Contact PA Bureau of Forestry, 717-424-3001; or National Park Service, South District Ranger Office NY Route 97, Pond Eddy, NY, 914-557-0222.

Mile 260.5: Knights Eddy Campground, c/o Landers River Trips (1336 Route 97, Narrowsburg, NY 12764, 914-252-3925 / 800-252-3925). NY Route 97 about 5 miles north of Port Jervis. Riverside tent sites and lean-tos, showers, camp store. Campers must be using Landers or privately owned river craft.

Mile 253.5: Tri-State Canoe Campground (Box 400 Shay Lane, Matamoras, PA 18336, 717-491-4948 / 800-56-CANOE). Off I-84 Exit 11, Routes PA 6 and US 209; by the Best Western Hotel. Riverside tent sites, showers, laundry.

Mile 249.7: River Beach Campsites (Route 209, Box 382, Milford, PA 18337, 717-296-7421 or -6030). On U.S. Route 209 3 miles north of Milford. Waterfront campsites, showers, camp store, laundry. Customers of Kittatinny Canoes river trips have priority for campsites. Campers going on the river must use Kittatinny or private canoes only.

Mile 236.2: Dingmans Campground (formerly Bernie's Camp-in) (RR 2 Box 20, Dingmans Ferry, PA 18328, 717-828-2266). Located on U.S. Route 209 .75 mile south of Route 739 intersection. From river: on PA side .5 mile south of Dingmans Bridge. April 15 through October 15. Reservations recommended. Operated as a concession under a permit from the National Park Service. Tent campsites at river edge, showers, camp store.

Mile 215: Worthington State Forest (HC 62 Box 2, Old Mine Road, Columbia, NJ 07832, 908-841-9575). On the Old Mine Road about 5 miles north of the Delaware Water Gap. April 1 through December 31. Sixty-nine riverside tent and trailer sites, 3 group campsites, showers. Operated by the New Jersey State Park Service.

Mile 204.1: Delaware River Campgrounds (US Route 46, Belvidere, NJ, 201-475-4517). Tent sites near river's edge.

Mile 170.0: Bucks County River Country campground, c/o Bucks County River Country (2 Walters Lane, Point Pleasant, PA 18950, 215-297-5000 / FAX: 215-297-5643). Tent sites near river's edge.

Mile 168 (approx.): Ringing Rocks Campground (75 Woodland Drive, Upper Black Eddy, PA 18972, 610-982-5552). Off Bridgeton Hill Road, Upper Black Eddy. About 1 mile from river. Tent sites, showers, laundry, camp store.

Mile 166.5: Dogwood Haven Family Campground (16 Lodi Hill Road, Upper Black Eddy, PA 18972, 610-982-5402). Located on Lock 19 of the Delaware Canal one block from the river. Just off PA Route 32. April 1 through November 1. Wooded campsites, hot showers. Operated by Delaware Canal State Park, PA.

Mile 163: Tinicum County Park (PA Route 32, Uhlerstown, PA). Vehicle access from PA Route 32 about 1.2 miles south of Uhlerstown-Frenchtown bridge; river access at Tinicum Park access area. Tent sites not far from river. Pit toilets.

Mile 156: Bulls Island Recreation Area (D&R Canal State Park, 2185 Daniel Bray Highway, Stockton, NJ 08559, 609-397-2949). On NJ Route 29 (Daniel Bray Highway) about 4 miles north of Stockton. Access from river at Bulls Island access, just downstream from Raven Rocks–Lumberville pedestrian bridge. April 1 through November 30. Seventy-five tent and trailer sites, shower and laundry available. Operated by the New Jersey State Park Service.

Mile 142: Washington Crossing State Park (355 Washington Crossing–Pennington Road, Titusville, NJ 08560, 609-737-0623). About 1 mile east of NJ Route 29 on Pennington Road. River access from Washington Crossing bridge. April 1 through October 30. Group camping only. Four sites with picnic tables, fire rings, pit toilets. Camping areas are about one mile from the river. Operated by the New Jersey State Park Service.

Public Access

Access	Mile
Balls Eddy (West Branch, PA)	335.3
Shehawken (West Branch, PA)	331.3
Buckingham (PA)	325.1
Long Eddy (NY)	315.5
Callicoon (NY)	303.6
Callicoon (PA)	303.1
Cochecton (NY)	298.5
Damascus (PA)	298.3
Skinners Falls (NY)	295.4
Narrowsburg (NY)	290.1
Narrowsburg (PA)	289.9
Zane Grey (PA)	277.6
Matamoras (PA)	256.1
Milford (PA)	246.2
Dingmans Ferry (PA)	238.5
Eshbeck (PA)	231.6
Bushkill (PA)	228.2
Depew Island (NJ)	221.3
Poxono (NJ)	220.0
Smithfield Beach (PA)	218.0
Worthington State Forest (NJ)	214.6
Kittatinny Point (NJ)	211.7
Portland (PA)	207.6
Portland Station (PA)	206.7
Martins Creek (PA)	194.2
Sandts Eddy (PA)	189.9
Phillipsburg (NJ)	184.0
Easton Front Street (PA)	183.7
Riegelsville (PA)	174.0
Upper Black Eddy (PA)	167.7
Kingman (NJ)	163.4
Tinicum County Park (PA)	162.9
Byram (NJ)	156.1
Bulls Island (NJ)	155.3
Lambertville (NJ)	148.6
Belle Mountain (NJ)	146.8
Yardley (PA)	138.7
Trenton Waterfront (NJ)	131.8

Rapids (I+ or More)

Mile	Name	Class
315.0	Long Eddy	I+
310.9	Hankins	I+
305.0	Hollister Creek	I+
295.2	Skinners Falls	II
286.6	(unnamed)	I+
285.0	RR Bridge No. 9	II–
284.0	Ten-Mile Rift	I+
282.0	Mast Hope Rift	I+
281.4	West Colang Rift	II
279.4	Narrows Falls (Kunkelli) Rift	II
277.4	Lackawaxen Rift	I+
276.7	Rock Rift	I+
275.0	Big Cedar Rift	II–
272.9	Shohola Rift	II
270.5	Buttermilk Falls	I+
266.9	(unnamed)	I+
263.3	Stairway Rift	I+
261.0	Mongaup Falls	II
260.0	Butlers Falls	I+
258.7	Sawmill Rift	I+
257.8	Glass House Rift	I+
248.8	Quicks Rift	I+
224.6	Mary and Sambo Rift	I+
209.0	Stony Brook Rift	I+
205.2	Anters Rift	I+
199.3	Buttermilk Rift	I+
196.7	Foul Rift	II
194.9	Capush Rift	I+
186.5	Hog Rift	I+
174.6	Rieglesville Rift	I+
158.3	Lotts Falls	I+
155.9	Raritan Dam	I+
148.0	Wells Falls	II/III
139.7	Scudders Falls	I+
134.1	Trenton Falls	I+
133.5	Trenton Falls (low tide)	II

Geological Features

Point Mountain (Hancock)	330.7
Skinners Falls (Milanville)	295.2
Hawks Nest (Sparrowbush)	260.0
Sawkill Falls (Milford)	246.2
Walpack Bend (Bushkill)	226.7
Delaware Water Gap	212.1
Slateford Farm Quarry	209.5
Terminal Moraine (Belvidere)	201.0
Foul Rift (Belvidere)	196.7
Palisades of the Delaware (Rieglesville)	171.9
Ringing Rocks (Upper Black Eddy)	169.0
New Jersey State Museum (Trenton)	134.4
Trenton Falls	133.5

Historical Features

Equinunk Historical Museum	322.5
Fort Delaware (Narrowsburg)	290.2
Roebling Bridge (Lackawaxen)	277.4
Battle of Minisink (Minisink Ford)	277.3
Erie Depot (Port Jervis)	254.7
Fort Decker (Port Jervis)	254.7
Pike County Historical Museum (Milford, PA)	246.1
Grey Towers (Milford, PA)	246.1
Old Mine Road (Flatbrookville)	233.5
Millbrook Village	223.5
Slateford Farm (Delaware Water Gap)	209.5
Easton Walking Tour	183.7
Hugh Moore Canal Museum (Easton)	183.6
Delaware Canal	183.6–134.5
Route 32 Inns	168.0–148.8
Irwin Stover House (Erwinna)	162.8
Delaware and Raritan Canal	156.0–139.5
David Library of the Revolution (Washington Crossing)	143.1
Washington Crossing	141.8
New Jersey State Museum (Trenton)	134.4
City of Trenton	133.5

Arts

Delaware Valley Arts Alliance (Narrowsburg) 290.0
Zane Grey Museum (Lackawaxen) 277.6
Peters Valley Crafts Village 238.5
Shawnee Playhouse (Shawnee-on-Delaware) 214.7
Hugh Moore Canal Museum (Easton) 183.6
Stover Mill (Erwinna) 162.3
Prallsville Mill (Stockton, NJ) 152.4
Bucks County Playhouse (New Hope) 148.3
Lambertville Flea Markets 146.7
Washington Crossing Theater 142.0
New Jersey State Museum (Trenton) 134.4

Bibliography

Beck, Henry Charlton. *Tales and Towns of Northern New Jersey.* New Brunswick, N.J.: Rutgers University Press, 1964.

Bowmans Hill Wild Flower Preserve Association. *Ways with Wild Flowers.* New Hope, Pa.: Bowmans Hill Wild Flower Preserve Association, 1983.

Cohen, David Steven. *The Folklore and Folklife of New Jersey.* New Brunswick, N.J.: Rutgers University Press, 1983.

Conference of Upper Delaware Townships. *Final River Management Plan*, Upper Delaware Scenic and Recreational River, 1986.

Corbett, Roger, and Fulcomer, Kathleen. *The Delaware River.* Springfield, Va.: Seneca Press, 1981.

Cunningham, John T. *New Jersey: America's Main Road.* Garden City, N.Y.: Doubleday & Company, 1966.

Curtis, Charles T. *Stories of the Raftsmen.* Callicoon, N.Y.: Town of Delaware Bicentennial Commission, 1976.

Curtis, Mary. *Rafting Tales.* Narrowsburg, N.Y.: Delaware Valley Arts Alliance, 1983.

Dale, Frank. *Delaware Diary.* New Brunswick, N.J.: Rutgers University Press, 1996.

Delaware and Raritan Canal Commission. *Delaware and Raritan Canal State Park Master Plan.* Trenton, N.J., 1977.

Fisher, Ronald M. *The Appalachian Trail.* Washington, D.C.: National Geographic Society, 1972.

Fluhr, George J. *A Generation of Suffering on the Upper Delaware Frontier.* Shohola, Pa.: reprinted from New-Eagle, Hawley, Pa., 1976.

Fluhr, George J. *Quarries, Kilgour, and Pike County, PA.* Milford, Pa.: Pike County Historical Society, 1984.

Henn, William F. *Westfall Township, Gateway to the West.* Milford, Pa.: Pike County Historical Society, 1978.

Hine, Charles Gilbert. *The Old Mine Road.* New Brunswick, N.J.: Rutgers University Press, 1963.

Hoff, J. Wallace. *Two Hundred Miles on the Delaware.* Trenton, N.J.: The Brandt Press, 1893.

Hungerford, Edward. *Men of Erie.* New York: Random House, 1946.

Kraft, Herbert C. *The Archeology of the Tocks Island Area.* South Orange, N.J.: Seton Hall University Museum, 1975.

Life Along the Delaware from Bushkill to Milford. Milford, Pa.: Pike County Historical Society, 1975.

McPhee, John. *In Suspect Terrain.* New York: Farrar, Straus & Giroux, 1982.

New York–New Jersey Trail Conference. *New York Walk Book.* Garden City, N.Y.: Doubleday/Natural History Press, 1971.

Punola, John A. *Canoeing and Fishing the Upper Delaware River.* Madison, N.J.: Pathfinder Publications, 1979.

Riviere, Bill. *Pole, Paddle, and Portage.* New York: Van Nostrand Reinhold Co., 1969.

Rivinus, Willis M. *A Wayfarer's Guide to the Delaware Canal.* Willis M. Rivinus, 1964.

Wakefield, Manville B. *Coal Boats to Tidewater.* South Fallsburg, N.Y.: Manville B. Wakefield, 1965.

Weiss, Harry B. *Rafting on the Delaware River.* Trenton, N.J.: New Jersey Agricultural Society, 1967.

Weslager, Clinton Alfred. *The Delaware Indians.* New Brunswick, N.J.: Rutgers University Press, 1972.

Widmer, Kemball. *The Geology and Geography of New Jersey.* Princeton, N.J.: D. Van Nostrand Co., 1964.

Index

About the Author

Gary Letcher for many years lived along the Delaware and guided many canoe trips on the river. He served as director of youth programs in the New Jersey State Park Service, and as an enforcement officer with the N. J. Division of Water Resources. Letcher lived in Alaska for several years, where he operated a canoe guide and livery business. He now lives with his wife, Shirley, and son, Ted, near Washington, D.C. He is kept busy by his environmental law practice when not toting his canoe to and from nearby rivers.